Portland Forest Hikes

PORTLAND
FOREST HIKES

TWENTY CLOSE-IN
WILDERNESS WALKS

James D. Thayer

TIMBER PRESS
Portland · London

Frontispiece: A trail through Portland's last remaining grove of old-growth firs beckons the hiker.

Facts stated in this book are to the best of the author's knowledge true, although bus routes and other specifics are subject to change without notice. The author and publisher can take no responsibility for the misidentification of mushrooms or plants by the users of this book nor for any illness that might result from their consumption. If there is any doubt whatsoever about the identity and edibility of a mushroom or plant, do not eat it. Users should exercise caution when hiking in wilderness areas; the maps in this book are as accurate as possible but limited in detail.

Maps by Erik Goetze, The Art of Geography
All photographs by James D. Thayer

Copyright © 2008 by James D. Thayer. All rights reserved.

Published in 2008 by
Timber Press, Inc.
The Haseltine Building
133 S.W. Second Avenue, Suite 450
Portland, Oregon 97204-3527, U.S.A.
www.timberpress.com

Designed by Susan Applegate
Printed in China

Library of Congress Cataloging-in-Publication Data

Thayer, James D.
    Portland Forest Hikes: Twenty close-in wilderness walks/James D. Thayer.
        p. cm.
    Includes bibliographical references and index.
    ISBN-13: 978-0-88192-857-0
    1. Trails—Oregon—Tualatin Mountains—Guidebooks. 2. Tualatin
Mountains (Or.)—Guidebooks. I. Title.
    GV199.42.O7T53 2008
    796.5209795—dc22   2007027205

To my parents

Charles W. Thayer and Cynthia Dunn Thayer,
who instilled in me a lifelong love of nature
and a passion for exploring the deep woods

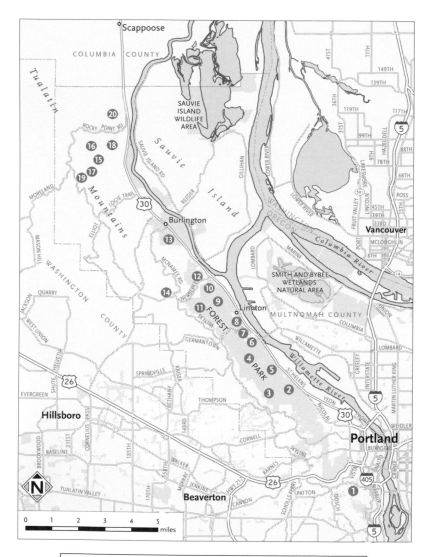

Contents

Acknowledgments

This book owes much of its inspiration to the pioneering work of Keith Hay. Keith's original vision of the Pacific Greenway remains firmly rooted in many of our minds and refuses to go away.

I am equally indebted to "Ding" Canon, Bill Keil, Thornton Munger, and C. Paul Keyser, all key contributors to the founding of Forest Park. I was honored to work with both Ding and Bill when I first joined what was then still called the Committee of Fifty. Their long-term determination gives me hope that great ideas can be realized in Oregon as long as you're patient and stubborn as hell.

And then there's Marcy Houle, whose wonderful *One City's Wilderness* provided the scientific backbone to the concept of a wildlife corridor. Without the inspiration to find out where that corridor went and how it functioned, I would still be happily puttering around the Hoyt Arboretum.

There are so many others who have helped me along the way and who I would like to thank. My wife, Cynthia, is foremost among them for her patience in putting up with my routine disappearing acts, which usually ended with heaps of muddy clothes and a filthy, exhausted Siberian husky whose first act upon returning home was to jump on the couch. A special thanks to my faithful companions Loki, Buddy, and Pal for accompanying me on my many expeditions, and to DoveLewis Emergency Animal Hospital for saving Loki's life after he was kicked by an elk.

My thanks go out to all those who helped me turn a jumble of ideas into a book, including the very talented editor Mindy Fitch. Without Eve Goodman's patience and encouragement at Timber Press, this book never would have been possible. Erik Goetze's lucid maps made the trails come alive in ways no amount of words could have achieved. I would like to thank Metro for helping me with many detail aerial maps, and David Bragdon in particular for helping me understand the regional scope of this project. Thanks, too, to Laura Foster for her review and contributions, and to Ian Hall for his evaluation of my information about mushrooms.

Finally there are the many nameless people upon whom I chanced while walking up these dusty roads, who told me about homesteading on Dixie Mountain, bootlegging in Linnton, and plenty of other fascinating stories. Oh, there's definitely gold out there in them hills if you can only listen! Thanks to all of you who added your intricate piece to the puzzle.

Introduction

The idea for this book originated in the 1990s. In 1992 Keith Hay, founder of the American Greenways Program, proposed a bold initiative called the Pacific Greenway project. It sought to establish three separate routes that would connect Forest Park with the Coast Range, thus protecting a major wildlife corridor while also providing a trail system through some of northwest Oregon's thickest forests in a part of the state that has received little recognition.

Imagine hiking trails from Portland to the Coast Range: it may some day be possible. This dream inspired this book of twenty wilderness hikes, each starting where the vision begins, closest to Portland. Certainly the more remote additions to our hiking repertoire are on the horizon as a growing population of hikers, runners, bikers, and equestrians continue to seek new venues for explorations in the northwest quadrant of Oregon.

Most modern cities are now surrounded by a wide belt of privately held, semi-developed lands that offer little opportunity for recreational access or enjoyment. Portland is unique in this respect. The northwest quadrant of the city is dominated by Forest Park, which is the basis for ten of the twenty trails in this volume. At 5000 acres it ranks as the largest natural urban forest reserve

The Jones Creek Hike: a 2-mile exploration into
the northern edge of Multnomah County

in the United States, stretching across 8 miles of wooded hillsides in the Tualatin Mountains. This sylvan peninsula extending into Portland offers tremendous hiking experiences, especially in the remoter areas described in this book. Concealed beyond it lie larger and more majestic woods that extend in a continuous forested carpet along the lower Columbia River all the way to the Pacific. Some of the most beautiful of these forests, with their labyrinthine networks of logging roads, are a mere thirty-minute drive from downtown Portland.

Basic guidance to the more accessible and popular trails of Forest Park, such as the Wildwood Trail and Leif Erikson Drive, is easy to come by. But there are dozens of other lesser-known urban trails that are literally off the beaten track and eminently worth seeking out for their quiet, undisturbed ambiance and for the rugged beauty of their natural settings. In addition to introducing these lesser-known trails inside Forest Park, this guide invites you into some rarely described prime Oregon hiking country that is nearly as close to Portland. The northern portion of the Tualatin Mountains, essentially a spur of the Coast Range that divides the Tualatin Valley from the Columbia River, is a treasure trove of close-in, accessible hikes of remarkable beauty and surprising remoteness, and is full of local cultural history. After more than four years of intensive exploration, research, Global Positioning System (GPS) mapping, and interviews with local residents, I am pleased to include nine hikes in the northern Tualatin Mountains.

Each chapter in this book begins with the essential information about each hike, including the trailhead location, distance covered by the hike, estimated duration, elevation changes, hiking conditions, and driving directions from the intersection of West Burnside and Interstate 405 in downtown Portland. As this book is primarily intended for urban hikers who want to experience relatively secluded forests near the city, I've also included information on how to access some of the closer trails using TriMet, Portland's regional bus service. For current bus schedules and routes, contact TriMet at 503-238-RIDE or visit www.trimet.org.

A detailed map of each hike follows the route through a series of waypoints that correspond to descriptions of points of special interest. These waypoints appear as **1**, **2**, **3**, and so forth. The first waypoint on each hike is the trailhead and parking location. Please use consideration when parking your vehicle. Gated roads should never be blocked, nor should you drive into any gated areas even if they are open. Keep in mind that a forester may be working inside the gated area. If he or she were to unknowingly lock you in, it would be a very unfortunate situation, especially since many of these areas do not have good cell phone reception.

Many of the remoter trails on these hikes are part of larger logging road networks that cover a much vaster area and are lots of fun to explore. Most of these other trails or logging roads are indicated in abbreviated form on each map to allow you to confirm your position along the way.

In estimating the duration of each hike, I've assumed a rate of travel of 2.5 miles per hour, a rather leisurely pace. A brisk walker could exceed 3 miles per hour, but such a pace would be too hurried to enjoy the environs.

Information on elevation changes should help you gauge how much climbing and descending is entailed for each hike, and the contour lines on the maps provide further details about local topography.

In my descriptions of hiking conditions I've tried to indicate the nature of the surface terrain, from gravel logging road to footpath to rugged track, paying particular attention to changing conditions due to inclement weather. Most of these trails and logging roads are easy to follow even if they are overgrown and not maintained, but a few of the more remote trails (Fire Lane 12 Loop,

Beaver Ponds Loop, Double Cross Loop, and Runaway Ridge Loop) include rudimentary tracks (either a game trail following a clearly discernable geographic contour, or a disused logging road) that provide a rough but strategic link in completing the loop.

A note about walking on logging roads versus trails: Logging roads run the gamut from green carpets of moss to rough-hewn roads surfaced with sharp, angular rocks. Many of the newly surfaced roads can be tough on the ankles, and you will want to wear hiking boots or other shoes with ankle support. But logging roads also have the benefit of being mostly dry (though occasionally muddy) even in wet weather, and in sunny weather they afford hikers exposure to sunlight and stunning vistas.

Accessibility to some of the less-frequented logging roads (especially undocumented side trails) may be an issue in some areas, especially at lower elevations where brambles are rampant. In general, however, the main element contributing to logging road congestion beyond Forest Park is alder tree proliferation, which is more of a nuisance than a real obstruction even with alders more than a decade old.

Where bushwhacking is required, such as on the Fire Lane 12 Loop and Double Cross Loop, I recommend bringing rose pruners, which are small and can cut brambles far better than any machete or hatchet. I do not recommend whacking away at brambles or alders with a hatchet; such an undertaking would be not only unnecessary but also dangerous and damaging to the forest. In private forests I would carry a hatchet only when fire rules require it; otherwise I strongly advise against carrying any implement that might be seen as posing a danger to the trees. During my own excursions I have used pruners on the Ennis Creek Hike, Double Cross Loop, and Jones Creek Hike. Otherwise I have generally found it easy enough to sidestep the brambles.

Each chapter describes some of the many plants and animals you are likely to see along these hikes. I also provide some of the fascinating history of each wilderness area, including accounts of local Indians and early settlers and descriptions of the rough-hewn communities they built. Where possible I have also included geological information.

Along the way I describe a sampling of the many mushrooms and plants often found along these hikes. Please note, however, that when it comes to identification you will need to consult other texts, as I am no expert. Although I grew up eating woodland mushrooms, I don't recommend doing so without a reliable reference in hand. Unfortunately it is very easy to confuse poisonous mushrooms and plants for edible ones, and the mistake can lead to serious illness or even death. Never under any circumstance eat any mushroom or plant unless you are very certain of its identity and edibility. Ian R. Hall and his coauthors provide the following sage advice at the beginning of *Edible and Poisonous Mushrooms of the World* (2003): "Even for a mushroom known to be edible, one should eat only a small amount the first time. Moreover, when eating wild mushrooms or new cultivated mushrooms, always place some uncooked ones aside in the refrigerator in case there has been a mistake or there is an allergic reaction to the mushroom." For more on identifying mushrooms in particular, consult references such as *Mushrooms of Northwest North America* (Schalkwijk-Barendsen 1994) or *National Audubon Society Field Guide to North American Mushrooms* (Lincoff 1981).

All but four of the hikes in this book are loops, meaning that the trail circles back along another route but returns you to the same starting point, presumably where you've parked your car. Where it was impossible to provide a looped route, the one-way trail has been designated simply as a hike. In the case of the Cable Trail to Rocky Point Road Hike, which is designed to be walked in one direction only, I've recommended parking a second car at the trail terminus.

While the names of established trails, public roads, and recognized streams are accurate, I have taken liberties with the naming of some of these hikes and the minor geographic features associated with them. The Cable Trail received its moniker from the presence of choker cables on the trail. Reference to the "elbow" curve on Skyline Boulevard, and the associated Elbow Ridge View Hike, derive from my personal description of this sharp bend in the road. My dog's occasional intractability gave rise to the name Runaway Ridge, and the Double Cross Loop is so named because it crosses two streams.

The first eleven hikes in this book take you through established parks in Southwest and Northwest Portland, while the last nine hikes wend their way through the more isolated slopes of the Tualatin Mountains.

Two hikes in the Tualatin Mountains, the Ennis Creek Hike and the Burlington Creek Loop, are located on property purchased by Metro. These areas have not yet officially been added to the roster of Metro parks, but since access is not explicitly prohibited, I have included them. We should maintain a light impact, however: Metro has limitations that prevent immediate development and is not promoting widespread use of these lands.

The remaining hikes in the Tualatin Mountains are located on private forestry land where limited recreational access is allowed, including daytime pedestrian use. On such land trees are grown, harvested, and replanted, resulting in a patchwork of bare logged ground, replanted slopes dotted with protectively encased seedlings, thick young forests, and stands of carefully thinned maturing trees. These large tracts of varying density constitute some the richest habitat for animals and provide rewarding walking for the dedicated hiker. These limited-access areas are clearly denoted by blue or orange gates usually accompanied by posted usage guidelines and a phone number for the land manager of the timber company. Please note that during the fire season (August through September) there may be limited or more extensive closures. In the case of a limited closure, hikers are allowed to enter but are asked to carry a shovel and a gallon of water. If conditions are more severe you may encounter a complete closure, which is usually posted at the entrance to the property. Check the Oregon Department of Forestry Web site for exact information about local closures: http://egov.oregon.gov/ODF/FIRE/precautionlevel.shtml. It is also a good idea to have a backup plan in case your favorite trail is closed. From time to time a timber company will close an area to all access when there is active logging, since logging is an inherently dangerous business.

Please don't litter, and observe the posted rules so that we may all continue to benefit from this privilege. Incidents of vandalism (a federal offense) have been especially unfortunate, both because of the very real danger they pose to loggers and because they can lead to the permanent closure of these beautiful privately managed forests for all of us. Of all the land I surveyed for this book, from the end of Forest Park all the way to the Nehalem River, managed timberland held the greatest concentration and variety of wildlife. Plentiful riparian areas separating different stages of forest maturity, improved habitat in thinned timber stands, and the preservation of local watersheds have all contributed to a marked increase in wildlife. By contrast, development of isolated private residences has clearly contributed to habitat degradation, the spread of invasive species, and a marked reduction in wildlife.

Ten million acres of Oregon's forests are privately owned and managed. Our hope of developing publicly accessible walking routes from Portland to the Oregon coast certainly depends in part on our ability to build effective relations with our state's private timber harvesters. As more recreational users gain exposure to Oregon's public and private forests, it should become clear that we all benefit from the healthy management of these forests.

Of course, always observe appropriate caution when it comes to fire and avoid any unnecessary disturbance of the flora and fauna, especially where restrictions are clearly posted about protecting local wildlife habitat.

A recreational-use notice

Cell phone reception is frequently unavailable in these remote areas, and access to these slopes is difficult by emergency vehicle or even on foot. It is a good practice to leave detailed information about your intended route and provide a finite check-in time, so that timely and focused search efforts can be initiated if necessary. Keep in mind, too, that diverging from your documented route will further complicate any search efforts.

Two final notes of caution and advice: First, the biggest danger in these woods is hypothermia, which initially manifests itself by impairing your judgment. Northwest woods are damp and cold. As a consequence they rob energy from your body, and the ensuing disorientation can leave you utterly lost in these complex networks of logging roads. Studies have shown that 99 percent of missing people who are found alive are discovered within the first fifty-one hours, with chances of survival diminishing rapidly after that. Don't fool yourself: this can happen as easily thirty minutes from home as it can on Mount Hood. Dress properly and stay dry. Should you get lost in any of these forests, don't adhere to the old Boy Scout adage about following water to civilization. That's the worst thing you could do here! Logging roads run along the tops of the hills, not along the bottom. The bottoms of our ravines are densely overgrown, wet, cold, and steep, leading only to more bodies of water. Climb to the ridgeline, where you will find the old logging roads. From there, keep looking for bigger, more recently used roads until you find the gate.

Having now warned against getting lost, I have to admit that this guidebook is at least partially the result of my passion for "losing" myself in the depths of our forests. I know that it's loopy and pointless, and even my dog doubts my sanity at times, but I can't stop mucking around in the woods. I usually arrive home many hours later, wet to the bone, with twigs sticking out of my

hair, my hat transformed into a soil-sample collector, and bramble scratches over every exposed inch of my body. Yet all week long I dream about wandering down long-abandoned logging roads. I recall the mists and fog sweeping up the valleys during my most recent visit and can't seem to stop wondering what was around that last bend in the road.

With this book I hope to bring you one step closer to sharing the thrill of spotting a coyote up ahead or being awestruck by the grace of a solitary "baldie" sweeping the sky above you. Perhaps one day we'll even meet somewhere very deep in the woods.

The shaggy parasol (*Macrolepiota rachodes*) is among the many mushrooms found in Oregon forests. Never consume any mushroom unless you are certain of its identity and edibility.

The bottoms of Oregon's ravines are cool and wet even in the heat of August but can be deadly for a disoriented hiker during the colder seasons.

21

Southwest Portland

Oregon grape *(Mahonia nervosa)*

① Marquam Nature Park Loop

TRAILHEAD SW Marquam Street, off Sam Jackson Park Road
DISTANCE 3 miles round trip
DURATION One hour and thirty minutes
ELEVATION A total change of 418 feet, with a low point of 300 feet and a high point of 718 feet
CONDITIONS This is a footpath. Portions of it can be muddy, but it is mostly graveled.

FROM DOWNTOWN This hike begins 2.2 miles from West Burnside and Interstate 405. Drive south on SW Broadway, past Portland State University and across Interstate 405. Turn left as you come off the bridge across Interstate 405. Turn right onto SW 6th Avenue; this turns into SW Sam Jackson Park Road beyond the next light. Proceed along Sam Jackson Park Road, passing the intersection with SW Terwilliger Boulevard. A short distance beyond that intersection, Sam Jackson Park Road bends sharply to the left and begins to ascend the hillside. In the curve you will see that an unmarked dirt road (SW Marquam Street) leads off to the right, ending in a small parking lot facing an interpretive shelter. This is the Marquam Nature Park shelter. Turn into this parking lot and park near the shelter.

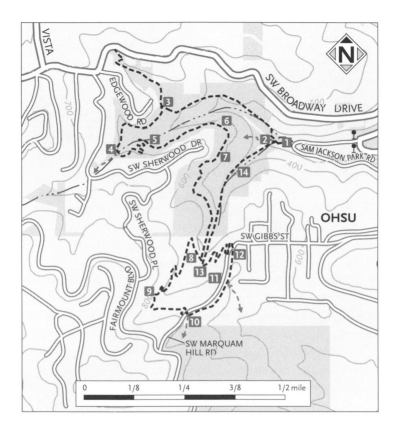

TriMet: From downtown, take bus 8 (Jackson Park) or 68 (Collins Circle), both of which travel to the intersection of Terwilliger Boulevard and Sam Jackson Park Road (bus stop 5804), the closest stop to the trailhead. Walk from the stop along Sam Jackson Park Road to the Marquam Nature Park shelter.

This trail ascends from the Marquam Nature Park shelter and traverses the two separate ravines in Marquam Gulch. At the head of the second ravine the trail rises to crest Marquam Hill Road before descending to a lower entrance and returning to the shelter. It's a reasonably easy hike and quickly accessible from downtown.

1 If you were to continue on Sam Jackson Park Road as it climbs Marquam Hill, you would soon reach Oregon Health and Science University (OHSU). Instead, as the road makes a 180-degree turn to ascend the hill, proceed straight onto Marquam Street.

2 The Marquam Nature Park shelter houses interesting historical information about the Marquam Gulch. It's worth stopping a few minutes here to take in the descriptions of the area's flora and fauna. Make sure to pick up a brochure on the Marquam Nature Park Loop; I'll refer to it later on this hike. The shelter also features a wonderful old water fountain with a special side dish that dogs can drink from. Dropping a stone in to cover the basin's drain will allow the water to collect sufficiently to slack your hound's thirst.

The origins of this area go back to its settlement in 1851 by John Talbot, who built his house at the base of this overgrown gulch. In 1875 Judge Philip A. Marquam, recently arrived from California, purchased the land in and around the ravine, including the hilltop that now houses OHSU, for $2750.

The base of the valley, lying south of a rapidly growing Portland, was the site of the city dump—situated approximately where Duniway Park is located today. The neck of the gulch above the dump soon became home to the most recent influx of immigrants, the Italians. Since most of the Tualatin Mountains had been extensively logged for firewood in the late 1800s, most of the vegetation in the gulch was dense and low, encouraging a thriving population of wild hogs. It is said that many Italian boys enjoyed

The Marquam Nature Park shelter

hunting these feral pigs, while older Italians scoured the hillsides for prized boletes, morels, and chanterelles.

After perusing the information at the shelter (elevation 300 feet), head up the hill along the short paved road. In about 10 feet you will see the beginning of the Sunnyside Trail branching off to the right. It crosses the floor of the valley just above the shelter, where you can still see the foundations of some of the early homes that dotted this area.

3 After ascending the northern flank of the gulch for about a quarter of a mile, you will reach a bench and a wooden staircase (elevation 530 feet) leading up to a spur that connects the trail system to SW Broadway Drive. A mile marker at this intersection allows you to gauge your progress, and the accompanying bench faces across the narrow valley, offering a deep-woods view of the Marquam Nature Park. It was the preservation of this undeveloped valley that led to one of Portland's earliest instances of neighborhood conflict with planned development. In 1969, neighbors and nearby residents banded together to successfully oppose a major development that was planned for this ravine. Fearing that the bucolic wilderness would be lost by the introduction of a multi-storied apartment building, they formed the Southwest Hills Residential League (SWHRL), one of the first neighborhood associations founded in the city.

Among the plants you'll encounter here and elsewhere on the hike is the Pacific rhododendron (*Rhododendron macrophyllum*). This magnificent shrub supplies the majority of the understory in the typical Northwest forest, providing dense foliage up to 15 feet in height. Along with vine maple, elderberry, hawthorn, and other midsized plants, the native rhododendron provides another stratum below what is found in the canopy and the emergent tree level. Its plain pink flowers add dramatic color to our monochromatic conifer forests.

Of course the other ubiquitous Oregon pathside plant is salal (*Gaultheria shallon*). The salal berry was among the most important food sources for Pacific Northwest Indians. Tribes along the Columbia River dried them in big cakes or loaves, stored them wrapped in skunk cabbage leaves (*Symplocarpus foetidus*), and ate them dipped in smelt oil. This berry, which ripens in late August, is one of the best in the woods—perhaps not as sweet as some, but full-flavored and perfect for jelly (especially after the tiny seeds are strained out).

4 About a third of a mile further, just past the next bench, the Sunnyside Trail intersects with the Marquam Trail. At this junction (elevation 610 feet) you are 0.25 mile from Sherwood Drive, which the Marquam Trail crosses as it ascends to Council Crest.

In 1974 a group of neighbors assembled 230 acres from donations and easements in the Marquam Gulch into what is now the Marquam Nature Park. By 1978 they had organized the Friends of Marquam Nature Park and built the first 12 miles of trails. In 2005 they added the Connor Trail, which connects OHSU to the Marquam Gulch.

If you wanted to extend this hike you could climb the Marquam Trail all the way to Council Crest (elevation 1073 feet). To the west of the summit, a trail leads down to the Oregon Zoo (via SW Talbot and SW Patton) and eventually connects to the Wildwood Trail. The Wildwood continues through Forest Park for more than 40 miles.

For now, instead of proceeding up the hill further, turn left onto the Marquam Trail and traverse the southern flank of the Marquam Gulch.

5 After dropping steeply downhill on a series of switchbacks, you will reach the intersection with the Shelter Trail (elevation 595 feet). Rather than continue downhill, continue straight on the Marquam Trail as it cuts across the flank of the hillside on a nice level path.

Keep a sharp eye open for evidence of woodpeckers as you walk along. Are the holes in the tree trunks round, or are they oblong? This will tell you much about who has been poking around.

One of the most dramatic woodpeckers to be seen in the Tualatin Mountains is the pileated woodpecker (*Dryocopus pileatus*). These spectacular crow-sized birds have long necks, white patches on their wings, and an unforgettable flaming red crest. They have a special fondness for carpenter ants, so they're often seen foraging low on dead trees or even on fallen logs. While not as common as northern flickers, they are clearly present, judging from the many oblong or square diggings they leave behind. Listen for the pileated woodpecker's loud, resonant single call of "wek" or "kuk." Sometimes he delivers a series of slow "kuk" calls in an irregular rhythm. His drumming (poking the tree) is slow, powerful, and irregular. Once you have seen a pileated woodpecker, you'll not likely forget this striking bird.

6 Continue for half a mile along the nearly level Marquam Trail as it follows the southern flank of the gulch around a ridge and into a little side valley.

7 As you proceed along this trail you'll notice numbered nature markers. These markers are explained in the Marquam Nature Park Loop brochure that was available at the shelter. Along the way you will also pass a narrow ravine that is bridged by a smooth log, a challenge for any surefooted youngster.

8 After passing half a mile along a beautifully wooded slope, the Marquam Trail intersects with the other end of the Shelter Trail in a narrow ravine. At this point the Shelter Trail is really a rough maintenance track that descends along the bottom of this side ravine down to the Marquam Nature Park shelter. You will not take this route at this time, however. Instead you will stop just short of the Shelter Trail intersection (marked by steps dropping to the floor of the ravine) and ascend the Upper Marquam Trail, which doubles back northward, climbing in 0.6 mile to Marquam Hill Road. The remote Upper Marquam Trail is a lovely, quiet, little-used portion of the park. A solitary bench graces one of the many switchbacks on the way up, affording a nice view of the ravine and the trails below.

9 Further up the ravine you might spot a coyote or two, which are known to inhabit this part of the park. Near the top of the valley you will cross the intermittent stream that flows down the ravine. Shortly thereafter the trail debouches onto Marquam Hill Road.

10 At 793 feet elevation you will reach Marquam Hill Road. Across the way is an abandoned logging road that partially penetrates the forested hillside below Fairmount Boulevard, commonly referred to as the Lakeman-Orkney property. In 2004 the City of Portland purchased this 45-acre parcel for $3.2 million. Together with lands owned by OHSU and the Three Rivers Land Conservancy, this large tract of steep, undeveloped woods is being preserved to form a large greenbelt around Marquam Hill. Some rudimentary trails meander through the undeveloped tracts, connecting with the Terwilliger Trail, which traverses the lower portions of the hillside. A new trail system is planned.

Proceed downhill along the Marquam Hill Road for about 100 yards, staying on the south (right) side of the road. As you pass a few homes on the left, you will see a large water storage tank.

Along the way you can see the beginning of the Terwilliger Trail on the right side of the road as it descends southward from Marquam Hill Road. This mile-long trail skirts the southern fringe of buildings and crosses a little creek that winds its way down to Terwilliger Boulevard. In 1996 Portland's largest landslide occurred in this area and obliterated part of this trail. Water seeped under Council Crest Drive until the land gave way, washing debris across Fairmount and into a steep ravine. Uprooted trees, mud, and debris repeatedly surged, dammed, and burst loose, eventually scouring the ravine and collecting on Terwilliger Boulevard.

11 After passing the Terwilliger Trail entrance, cross the road to the water tank. Immediately beyond the tank is the starting point for the Marquam Trail. From behind the western guard rail on Marquam Hill Road (elevation 718 feet), the Marquam Trail descends steeply into the ravine, where it reaches the top of the Shelter Trail (elevation 505 feet).

12 From this upper end of the ravine, you will follow the sometimes-muddy Shelter Trail along the creek for 0.4 mile to the base of the Marquam Gulch and the Marquam Nature Park shelter.

13 On the way you will pass the steps that mark the junction of the Marquam and Shelter trails. Above and to the left you should see the section of the Marquam Trail that you followed on the way up and the switchback you took to ascend to the top of the ravine.

As you hike down the Shelter Trail, note the basalt peeking out from under the tree roots to the right. This is the substrate of the Tualatin Mountains. Especially in this area, the covering soil is very unstable and continues to slide off whenever the ground gets too wet (which in Oregon is quite often). One sure sign of soil instability is the presence of so-called pistol-grip trees, whose trunks are curved at the base. These trees graphically illustrate the struggle between the vertical tree growth and the hillside's lateral movement.

14 Just before you reach the end of the Shelter Trail you will pass the Connor Trail ascending the hillside to the right. This more recent addition to the Marquam Nature Park trail system rises about 290 feet in less than a third of a mile as it leads up to the OHSU campus.

OHSU's 116-acre Marquam Hill campus first got its start in 1915 when Dr. Kenneth A. J. Mackenzie persuaded the Oregon-

Washington Railroad and Navigation Company that putting a switching yard atop Marquam Hill was a bit of a stretch, and that it was better suited for a medical school.

Mackenzie persuaded the railroad to donate a 20-acre tract and convinced the family of C. S. Jackson, former publisher of the *Oregon Journal*, to donate another 88 acres. However, others thought that building a medical school on a mountain accessible only by steep wagon road was as improbable as a switching yard; they scoffed at the notion, calling it Mackenzie's Folly. Ironically, the issue of access continued to bedevil this site in 2005 as OHSU and the City of Portland struggled to finance the Portland Aerial Tram, which improved access to the hilltop medical facility from SW Gibbs Street in the newly developed South Waterfront district.

Northwest Portland

St. Johns Bridge

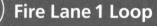

② Fire Lane 1 Loop

TRAILHEAD North side of 4315 NW St. Helens Road
DISTANCE 4.9 miles round trip
DURATION Two hours and thirty minutes
ELEVATION A total change of 880 feet, with a low point of 50 feet and a high point of 930 feet
CONDITIONS The lower portions of this trail can be muddy in the wet seasons, but mostly the trail is a stony roadway with steep inclines. There is some evidence of homeless bivouacking near the trailhead on St. Helens Road.

FROM DOWNTOWN This hike begins 3.6 miles from West Burnside and Interstate 405. Travel north on Highway 30 (also called St. Helens Road). Drive past the Burlington Northern/Southern Pacific rail yard all the way to the intersection with NW Kittridge Avenue and St. Helens Road. Turn left, heading south on St. Helens Road. Immediately after entering this road, pull off to the right beside the chain-link fence at Brazil Electric Motors (4315 NW St. Helens Road). Along the north side of this business you will see an undeveloped parcel with a dirt track ascending the wooded hillside. That's the trailhead.

    TriMet: From downtown, take bus 17 (NW 21st Avenue/St. Hel-

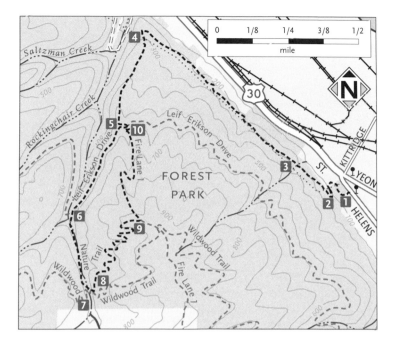

ens Road) and disembark at NW Yeon and Kittridge (bus stop 5337).

ALTERNATE ROUTE If you prefer to enter this hike from the top, here's how to access the trailhead on Fire Lane 1: Head east on NW Lovejoy Street, which turns northward after NW 25th Avenue and becomes NW Cornell Road. Follow this scenic road through the tunnels and up the Balch Creek Canyon. The second right turn (after the Audubon Society of Portland) is NW Thompson Road. Follow this road for about a mile, and turn into NW 53rd Drive. Immediately after entering 53rd, look for a long driveway on the left. Drive straight up this road. Various homes have access via this road, but it soon turns into a pothole-riddled dirt road that penetrates the park for quite a distance. Park at the end, near the gate, and enter the park. The upper portion of Fire Lane 1 is fairly level, meandering through a grove of quite tall Douglas firs before descending 100 feet in elevation and crossing the Wildwood Trail. Continuing on another 100 yards will lead you to the meadow mentioned in waypoints 9 and 10.

I often walk this trail when time is short and the sky (at least at lower elevations) is clear enough that I can enjoy panoramic views of North Portland, Swan Island, and the industrial portion of Northwest Portland that shares the horizon with Mount Hood. Mount St. Helens and Mount Adams are also clearly visible to the north, as is much of the commercial river and rail traffic that throngs this part of town. This neighborhood has a gritty kind of beauty, and the Fire Lane 1 Loop allows you to gaze down over it from the solitude of a remote forested trail.

1 The lower end of Fire Lane 1 begins at the junction of St. Helens Road and Yeon Avenue. The trail can be accessed from the lot just north of Brazil Electric Motors on St. Helens Road. At the back end of that lot you'll spot a rough track curving to the right up the slope. Follow the track 50 feet further up the slope, and the trail turns left and climbs steeply uphill for another 50 feet.

This is definitely among the least-traveled trails at the southern end of Forest Park. Not for long, though: Portland Parks and Recreation plans to build a park entrance here that will undoubtedly increase the traffic on this seldom-used trail. This access point also serves some of the transient community who make their homes in the lower portions of Forest Park during the warmer months. I've never encountered any denizens "living rough," but I've stumbled across at least a half-dozen camps located along the several noticeable side trails.

Despite the clandestine camps, this trail offers hidden beauty that is well worth the steep climb—and steep it is, rising from about 50 feet in elevation to over 900 feet in less than 2 miles. You may encounter a mountain biker or two, but runners typically eschew such a slope.

2 Just above the entrance the trail doubles back and begins to head north. Ignore the paths heading south and proceed north on the trail, which parallels a local set of power lines and an impenetrable blackberry thicket on the left. Over the first half mile the trail rises from 50 feet to about 300 feet, dipping back to 200 feet in the second half-mile stretch. All the time you're skirting the very bottom of the thickly wooded slopes of lower Forest Park, an area rich in wildlife.

No other American city has as large a contiguous urban park as Portland, and none can boast a wildlife corridor that allows beavers, coyotes, hawks, and deer—and sometimes even bears, cougars, and elk—to wander into the urban fabric. Portland Parks and Recreation has taken pains to slow and reverse the growing pressure of urbanization on this corridor, resisting development of private parcels inside the park and restricting the development of most of the trail system to the slopes above Leif Erikson Drive. As a consequence the lower elevations, such as this portion of the hike, constitute the main habitat area for larger mammals in the park.

3 This rising and dipping trail is one of the few that traverses these secluded slopes. As you follow it northward, take care to keep your eager hound from bounding up the slope after the delicious scent of elusive deer.

4 This lower portion of the trail comes to an abrupt halt about a mile from the start, at a promontory directly above Saltzman Road. To the north of this promontory is a steep valley that accommodates Saltzman Creek and Saltzman Road.

In the summer of 2004, during one of my periodic bushwhacking adventures, I had an interesting experience on Saltzman Creek. Following human tracks up the creek, I discovered occasional examples of artistry at work in the wilds: stream rocks had been carefully cemented together to form little cairns over the brook. Eventually I came to a rudimentary rock dam that produced a lovely small pool. Below the pool an elaborate stone castle of cemented rocks sat athwart the stream, and a hammock stretched above. A little way up the slope I could just barely make out a dwelling built into the hillside. A cozier hideaway couldn't be imagined! I left this sylvan Shangri-la as quietly as I had entered.

Later that same summer, park rangers raided the illegal, half-buried dwelling and found a man and his daughter living there. It took the rangers and teams of work-release laborers a week to haul 4800 pounds of material from this impromptu home in the Saltzman ravine. The police officer presiding over the dismantling of the camp offered the man and his daughter shelter on a ranch, but they disappeared a week later. It's quite possible that they're back in the park, perhaps more deeply hidden this time.

From the promontory above Saltzman Creek, the trail takes a sharp turn to the left and for the next half mile climbs steadily through a mature stand of mixed hemlock and Douglas fir until it reaches Leif Erikson Drive. From its start to its intersection with

Leif Erikson, this route ascends more than 550 feet in elevation within 1.5 miles; it should take about forty-five minutes to climb.

5 From the Leif Erikson gate, turn right and enjoy a leisurely stroll along Leif Erikson Drive. This meandering road, which traverses the Tualatin Mountains at about 600 feet elevation, was built in 1910 by land developer Richard Shepherd. He had hoped to encourage a large-scale development and laid out a vast number of lots across the hillside, but the expected land boom never materialized, and eventually these properties were forfeited to the city. In the end the city acquired some 1400 acres, and more were later relinquished to city ownership after being logged.

This is one of the nicest stretches of Leif Erikson Drive, especially as it offers clear, open vistas across the wooded forest. On the left you'll see the great walls of basalt that form the bedrock of this area.

6 Follow the road (not quite so heavily trafficked at this point) for about a quarter of a mile to the back of the valley, where Leif Erikson Drive doubles back to continue on its northward route. Here you'll find two small streams converging from parallel ravines. A trail runs up each stream: the Nature Trail ascends the left fork, while the Chestnut Trail climbs the right fork.

For a slightly longer walk you could take the Chestnut Trail, a pretty little trek that ascends a narrow ravine to join the Wildwood Trail another 300 feet higher up the slope. From there the Wildwood Trail leads southeast to where it intersects with Fire Lane 1.

This hike, however, follows the shorter route and ascends the Nature Trail. This lovely meandering trail is somewhat oddly named—it certainly has lots of nature on display, but as to why it's more natural than the other trails, it beats me!

If you keep a sharp eye open you might spot a creamy white mass attached to the base of a conifer. Looking like a compact pile of noodles from 6 inches to 3 feet in diameter, the cauliflower mushroom (*Sparassis crispa*, synonym *S. radicata*) can weigh as much as 50 pounds.

7 As you walk further up the Nature Trail, paralleling the small creek, you can't avoid spotting numerous sword ferns, which Northwest Indians called the pala-pala plant. Indian children would see how many leaflets they could pull off a stem, while saying "pala" for each one. The stems were used as protective layers in pit ovens, food storage boxes, and on berry-drying racks, and

Cauliflower mushroom (*Sparassis crispa*)

were even used for flooring and bedding. These larger sword ferns were also gathered in early spring by many coastal tribes and set aside as starvation food.

Further up the ravine and closer to the water you will find my favorite fern, the lovely maidenhair. This fern, with its few black stems and palmately branched leaflets, grows in very moist, shady, rocky sites, often near the spray of waterfalls. I love to let my hand brush through soft colonies of maidenhair ferns as they cluster alongside some misty corner of a ravine. Apparently the name derives from either the dark, hairlike stems or the tangle of dark root hairs at their base. In Europe this delicate fern was traditionally mixed with sugar to make an emetic cough syrup called *capillaire*. Pacific Northwest Indians used it in a drink to promote strength for dancers. It was also used in basketry by some tribes in Washington.

8 Shortly after the Nature Trail turns to climb up and away from the small brook, it intersects with a short connector trail that allows access to the Wildwood Trail, which passes close by. The Wildwood Trail parallels the Nature Trail and connects with Fire Lane 1 further up the slope. We will not take this branch but will continue along the Nature Trail, paralleling the Wildwood Trail above.

9 Eventually, after much winding in and out of small ravines, the Nature Trail emerges into a small meadow. Walk to the top of the meadow and above you will see Fire Lane 1 descending into the park from 53rd Drive. To the left you will see Fire Lane 1 continue down the slope.

At the crest of the hill above you is the northern edge of the Balch Creek watershed. This is one of the most heavily protected watersheds in the Portland area. Since 1989, when it became apparent that stringent efforts were needed to preserve this unique natural area in Portland's urban core, enormous efforts have been made to limit development and restore critical habitat along Balch Creek. Old-growth giants still tower above Cornell Road, and Balch Creek boasts its own landlocked population of cutthroat trout. But things were not always thus . . .

One of the most infamous tales of nefarious doings in Forest Park played out in this very valley. In 1905 Lafe Pence, a developer recently arrived from Denver, concocted an audacious plan to level a large tract of land between Macleay Park and Willamette Heights. The plan was to sluice off a large terraced area for residences and to wash the soil down into Guilds Lake, which was located between what is now St. Helens Road and Yeon Avenue.

Unbeknownst to anyone, the enterprising Mr. Pence managed to build over 6000 feet of an elaborate system of aqueducts and ditches that supplied water to his hydraulicking operations inside Macleay Park. To supplement the flow of Balch Creek, he even tunneled under the Skyline Ridge of the Tualatin Mountains to tap streams flowing down the western slope. Along the northern slope of Balch Creek he built a 4-foot-wide wooden flume that was sufficient to flush the entire seasonal flow of Balch Creek down the hillside and into Guilds Lake. All of this enormous construction occurred secretly and without anyone's permission. Finally one Sunday in late February of 1906, the agent of the neighboring property discovered Pence's surreptitious project and brought the encroachment to the attention of Mayor Harry Lane. The mayor and a police squad armed with sledgehammers soon wrecked over 20 feet of the massive flume, spelling the failure of yet another developer's dream to exploit this pristine wilderness so close to the city.

Remnants of the ditch system can be seen along the Wildwood Trail just a mile north of where the Wild Cherry Trail intersects with the Wildwood, or about 3 miles south of Fire Lane 1.

10 Follow Fire Lane 1 down to your left. It's a short walk down from the meadow to the gate on Leif Erikson that you recently passed as you ascended. Approximately thirty-five minutes should have elapsed since you passed through this gate on your way up the trail. Another forty-five minutes are required to descend from the gate to Highway 30, the start of the hike.

3 Fire Lane 3 and Upper Maple Trail Loop

TRAILHEAD 4040 NW Skyline Boulevard, near Thunder Crest Drive

DISTANCE 4.5 miles round trip

DURATION Two hours and thirty minutes

ELEVATION A total change of 476 feet, with a low point of 661 feet and a high point of 1137 feet

CONDITIONS This hike is a steep grade, and slippery when wet, but beautiful in the fog.

FROM DOWNTOWN This hike begins 6.3 miles from West Burnside and Interstate 405. Drive west on NW Lovejoy Street until it turns into NW Cornell Road. Turn right onto NW Thompson Road and right again onto NW Skyline Boulevard. Proceed northward for 0.6 mile. Look for the entrance to the Thunder Crest development on Thunder Crest Drive, branching off to the right. Don't park in the development, but park along Skyline Boulevard or across the street near the subdivision on the west side of Skyline.

This is among my favorite places to hike in the fog and rain. The trail is pretty good overall, and it is a relatively accessible, close-in walk, with little traffic on all but the Wildwood Trail segment. Amidst tall stands of Douglas fir, this trail affords mysteri-

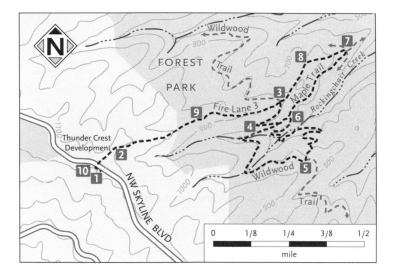

ous glimpses down the slopes between the stately trunks and into the deep forest below. The portion of the Wildwood that heads south to Fire Lane 2 twists in and out of deep ravines with at least two really impressive older-growth Douglas firs standing along-side the trail, each with a diameter in excess of 6 feet! The Upper Maple Trail sports a beautiful mixed-conifer forest. Hemlock, cedar, Douglas fir, and vine maple present a brilliant panorama in the fall.

1 The sign at the entrance to the Thunder Crest development points out that it is a private road, but you may walk through it to reach the trailhead at the eastern side of the development.

2 Having walked the short distance down Thunder Crest Drive, you will see a park gate on the right. This is Fire Lane 3. This fire lane is basically a long, straight, steep drop into the park. It is pretty well maintained and hasn't yet developed the characteristic V-shape that results from overuse by bicyclists.

3 At an elevation of 895 feet, Fire Lane 3 intersects with the Wildwood Trail before proceeding further down to Leif Erikson Drive. Here you will turn right, heading south on the Wildwood Trail.

A word of caution about the Wildwood Trail: On a sunny weekend expect to have to stand aside for long trains of huffing runners, as many as ten to fifteen in a row. You can hear them coming as the forest reverberates to their calls of "root," "rock," and "runner up" as the leader warns of obstacles ahead. If you're walking a dog, I suggest pulling him off the trail to allow for smooth passage. Keep your puppies leashed, too, especially if they're inclined to follow people, or you too will be joining the bobbing queue. On a nice day expect to encounter as many as ten or more trains of trotting runners between Fire Lane 3 and Fire Lane 2, most of them heading north.

4 Although this loop is designed to connect to the top of the Maple Trail, a shortcut is available about 100 yards along the Wildwood Trail. Here a short connector trail drops down from the Wildwood to the Maple Trail. This shortcut will abbreviate the walk by about a mile but will omit the old-growth trees and the upper portion of the Maple Trail.

Given that the hikes in this book are intended to avoid the traffic on the Wildwood Trail, you may wonder why this trail is included in the selection. Actually, the original trail descended into Forest Park on Fire Lane 2, but a private developer has since closed this access point.

Not only does this closure represent a significant loss for hikers in the park, it also poses some considerable public safety issues. Fire Lane 2 provides access to the exact location where one of the park's worst fires was sparked. It was built after the infamous Bonny Slope fire burned over 1000 acres of forest in 1940, beginning in the park but quickly jumping over Skyline Boulevard and engulfing the western hillside down to the settlement of Bonny Slope. At that time the area was mostly lightly forested land with few residences. Today the area is part of Forest Heights and is thickly populated, with many expensive residences at risk.

It is worth noting that after the ineffective response by Portland fire teams, City Hall was assailed by a political "firestorm." Eventually this led to the building of fire lanes across the park and annual forest fire training for Portland's firefighters.

Loki on Fire Lane 3

The danger of a forest fire hasn't fundamentally diminished since 1940; indeed, it may have grown in view of the increased fuel load (amount of potentially combustible material) in the park today. With summers becoming increasingly dry and more people entering the park, the risk that we might experience another conflagration like the Bonny Slope fire is not inconceivable. Without access to Fire Lane 2 the consequences could be dire.

5 If you ignore the shortcut and proceed along the Wildwood Trail for another 1.5 miles as it twists in and out of ravines, you will encounter a turnoff on the left that marks the beginning of the Maple Trail. Turn at this junction (which occurs just before Wildwood crosses Fire Lane 2) and proceed along the Maple Trail as it meanders down toward Leif Erikson Drive. About a quarter of a mile down the trail you'll spot Leif Erikson below you. Close as it may seem, that isn't where you're going. The trail heads back up the draw and crosses Rockingchair Creek before heading north over the next ridge. Nearly a mile later the Maple Trail deposits you on Leif Erikson, well beyond the bend that was spotted previously.

6 After crossing Rockingchair Creek and climbing the hill to parallel Leif Erikson Drive, you will encounter the lower end of the shortcut mentioned earlier. This stretch of the Maple Trail along the south-facing side of the Rockingchair Creek valley is particularly scenic, a beautiful mixed-conifer forest with hemlock, cedar, and Douglas fir sharing the hillside. The ground cover is predominantly sword ferns and Oregon grape (*Mahonia nervosa*), which turns a brilliant red in late fall. Oregon grape is perhaps the most common ground cover to be found in the Oregon woods.

In western Oregon the dull variety of Oregon grape can be found in second-growth, closed-canopy Douglas fir forests. The tart purple berries of this plant were eaten by Indians, though not in great quantities. Frequently they were mixed with salal berries or some other sweeter fruit. The bark and berries were also used medicinally for liver, gallbladder, and eye problems, and the yellowish bark was used to color basket materials. Today, some people make wine from these berries, but more often they are used to make a jelly mixed with an equal portion of salal berries.

7 Arriving at Leif Erikson Drive, you now begin to ascend Fire Lane 3, which also intersects with Leif Erikson at this point. Although you will climb almost 500 feet in the next 2.15 miles, this fire lane has many gently rising slopes to break up the steep bits. The forest here is mostly hemlock and alder, and the trail is quite straight, giving the impression that you're walking up a long sylvan corridor.

8 On these upper slopes, which are a relatively open conifer forest, you're likely to see lots of mushrooms, including those belonging to the genus *Tricholoma*. The most common *Tricholoma* species that I've espied while traipsing these hills are the streaked tricholoma (*T. portentosum*) and sulphur tricholoma (*T. sulphureum*). Though both are common, neither is worth picking for dinner, especially since this genus includes other less palatable brethren. I stay away from genera of mushrooms with a mixed gastronomic heritage: the rewards of the few marginally edible varieties do not outweigh the indigestibility of the rest.

9 Lifting your gaze as you ascend this fire lane, you will see that you're entering middle-aged Douglas fir stands that cover the upper hillsides on either side of this ridgetop road, affording intriguing glimpses deep into the forest.

In late March and early April, keep an eye open for the ubiquitous trillium with its telltale three white or pink petals. For me this iconic flower of the Northwest is the first harbinger of spring, its cheery white petals foretelling of some distant day when the rains will actually cease. The oft-repeated injunction about not picking trilliums because they may then take seven more years to reappear is a myth, although removing the seeds will certainly not help its propagation. In any case, resist the temptation to pick these flowers wherever you may find them, keeping in mind that as the population continues to grow in the Portland area it behooves us all to tread ever more lightly to retain the health and diversity of close-in wilderness areas.

The Indians cultivated an even less credible myth, but one more likely to occur. Pick a trillium, Quinault children were warned, and it will rain.

The trillium is noteworthy for yet another reason: it owes its existence to the messy habits of the ants who feed upon the gummy oil that encases its seeds. Once the seeds are stripped of this yummy covering, the ants ditch them along with the rest of their ant garbage, and presto, the trillium is distributed throughout the forest.

10 At the upper end of Fire Lane 3 you emerge from the forest and reenter the development on Thunder Crest Drive. At this point you're at an elevation of nearly 1130 feet, and from the far side of Skyline Boulevard you can survey the entirety of the Forest Heights housing development on the western slope of the Tualatin Mountains.

As you contemplate the dense housing just over the crest and even along the top of the Tualatin Mountains, you might wish to mentally thank some of the farsighted individuals without whose dedication Forest Park would never have been preserved and protected.

In particular we should remember Thornton Munger, "Ding" Canon, and Bill Keil, who spearheaded the efforts to establish the park. Immediately after the formal establishment of Forest Park in 1948, Thornton and his conservation-minded colleagues formed the Committee of Fifty, a group dedicated to the park's maintenance and preservation. For years the committee met in the famed Forestry Building, which sadly burned down in 1964. In 1983, when I first contacted the Committee of Fifty, the final dozen or so members were still meeting regularly at City Hall, carrying on the vision of a progressively managed urban forest. By the mid-1980s a new generation of urban environmentalists was serving as the stewards of Forest Park. In 1988 local activist Marcy Houle published *One City's Wilderness,* which suggested that the vitality of Forest Park was due in large part to the existence of a wildlife corridor that sustained the species diversity in the park. Anecdotal evidence of large animals threading their way into Portland from the Coast Range seemed to support the existence of a kind of natural underground railroad that allowed populations of imperiled animals to avoid isolation and extinction.

At the same time a proposed freeway through the park galvanized legions of environmentally minded Portlanders to fund the Friends of Forest Park's newly established campaign to purchase a threatened parcel of old-growth trees and various privately held parcels inside the park. No longer viewing the park as a laboratory for progressive forestry, the new leadership saw the park as a cultural treasure that required protection from the pressures of urbanization. The Friends of Forest Park continues to be a very active environmental group, helping to maintain this extraordinary treasure and supporting the expansion of protected greenspaces throughout the Portland area.

4 Trillium and Hardesty Trails Loop

TRAILHEAD East fork of NW Springville Road and Skyline Boulevard

DISTANCE 3.4 miles round trip

DURATION Two hours

ELEVATION A total change of 130 feet, with a low point of 850 feet and a high point of 980 feet

CONDITIONS Most of this hike follows the Wildwood Trail, which can be muddy in winter. However, since this portion of the Wildwood is well removed from most of the popular access points, the traffic is lighter and the mud factor somewhat less. Trillium Trail, which runs between Fire Lane 7 and the Wildwood Trail, is a short, lightly marked path, but once located it is easy to follow. Although it descends in twists and turns, it should pose little difficulty. Alternatively the hike can be shortened by using Fire Lane 7 to connect to or from the Wildwood Trail. The Hardesty Trail, which leads from the Wildwood Trail back up to the top of the ridge, was chosen because it has been improved and has lots of reinforced steps in all the right places.

FROM DOWNTOWN This hike begins 10 miles from West Burnside and Interstate 405. Drive west on NW Lovejoy Street until

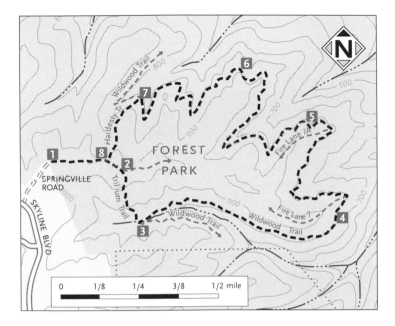

it turns into NW Cornell Road. Turn right onto NW Thompson Road and right again onto NW Skyline Boulevard. Proceed northward past the cemetery, past NW Saltzman Road, and just past the intersection with NW Springville Road on the left. Proceed up the hill, and as Skyline curves to the left, turn right onto Springville Road—a dirt road at this point. You will find good parking near the Springville Road gate.

This pleasant midpark walk traverses a long ridge along which Fire Lane 7 descends into the park. Though the hike encircles the ridge, you can choose to either descend or return up the ridge to shorten the walk. Fire Lane 7 is a lovely hike in the fall, as the trees arch over the trail to form a verdant cathedral effect.

1 The parking lot is located on Springville Road, one of the original tracks across the Tualatin Mountains. Both the Ridge Trail Loop and Willalatin Ridge Loop are also accessed by or partially use Springville Road.

Proceed past the gate on Springville Road and along the ridgetop following Fire Lane 7. This is a very pleasant (and mostly level) fire lane. Overhanging groves of alder trees give it the feel of a long, wooded corridor.

The first trail that you encounter will be the Hardesty Trail, which climbs up to join Fire Lane 7 from the left. Continue on past this trail; you will return by this route on the final leg of the hike.

Trilliums

2 Almost immediately beyond this trailhead (0.2 mile from the parking lot) you will see a small unmarked trail heading off to the right, just before the red-striped marker for the gas line. This is the Trillium Trail, which you will use to reach the Wildwood Trail. The Trillium Trail is clear enough to follow down the slope, but it is narrow, with lots of overhanging limbs and many twists and turns. A quarter of a mile later you will emerge at Doane Creek, where the Trillium joins the Wildwood Trail.

Walking the Tualatin Mountains provides frequent opportunities to appreciate the many varieties of edible berries found in western Oregon. From late May through the end of September these woods offer a constant progression of ripened berries to snack on. During late July and August I've frequently been able to find (and eat) as many as six different varieties of ripe berries, including huckleberries, thimbleberries, blackberries, salmonberries, wild raspberries, and salal berries. Even my dog Loki has come to appreciate these treats and in late summer can be observed snuffling through the blackberries to see if they are ripe yet.

The season's first berry is usually the huckleberry, which begins to ripen in June. Growing in the shade of deep forest cover, huckleberries are expansive bushes with small leaves. They can produce a range of fruit from prolific to sparse depending upon the growing conditions and seasonality. The deeper the shade, the fewer the berries you're likely to find, but even a few huckleberries make a special treat for an appreciative walker. In general these berries are mildly tart and especially well suited for jam or preserves.

Among the most frequently spotted berries, and one of my favorites, is the delicious thimbleberry (*Rubus parviflorus*). This berry sits on its stem like a crimson cap, readily popping off when ripe. The consistency is pastier than the juicy blackberry, but the flavor is more intense than a strawberry. This humble berry has a more prosaic value as well: its leaves are big, broad, and velvety, making them an ideal substitute for soft paper should the need arise far away from civilized amenities.

3 At the point where the Trillium Trail meets the Wildwood Trail, turn left and follow the trail eastward for about a mile to the end of the ridge. This trail, which skirts along the south-facing slope of the ridge, passes through some pleasant stands of nearly mature timber. Halfway along the slope you'll traverse a buried gas line crossing.

Keep an eye open for the mourning dove (*Zenaida macroura*), one of the most ubiquitous birds of the Tualatin Mountains. This slender gray dove is recognized by its long, tapered, white-tipped tail as well as by its mournful song: listen for its "ooahh . . . coo . . . coo . . . coo" or quavering "poooo" coming through the trees. Like its cousin the pigeon, this dove drinks up to 15 percent of its body-weight on a daily basis, sucking the water directly into its esophagus rather than dipping its beak into the water and letting it roll down its throat as is common among all other birds.

4 At the eastern end of the ridge you'll pass the junction with Fire Lane 7 (Oil Line Road). If you want to shorten this hike you can ascend Fire Lane 7 all the way back to the parking lot on Springville Road.

5 Half a mile later you'll pass the junction with Fire Lane 7a (Gas Line Road).

6 A further mile will bring you to the intersection with the Ridge Trail junction. This trail also drops all the way down to the St. Johns Bridge and is described in another hike: the Ridge Trail Loop.

7 Finally, after 3 miles of winding around this long ridgeline, you'll return to the lower end of the Hardesty Trail. Along the way you can often see some of the repairs made to areas of the trail damaged by heavy winter rains. Ascend the Hardesty Trail for about half a mile to where it meets Fire Lane 7.

8 At the intersection of the Hardesty Trail and Fire Lane 7, turn right to return to the Springville Road gate.

5 Saltzman Road and Lower Maple Trail Loop

TRAILHEAD NW Saltzman Road, 0.7 mile off St. Helens Road
DISTANCE 2.6 miles round trip
DURATION One hour and ten minutes
ELEVATION A total change of 407 feet, with a low point of 249 feet and a high point of 656 feet
CONDITIONS This easily accessible loop can be walked briskly or at a civilized amble.

FROM DOWNTOWN This hike begins 5.3 miles from West Burnside and Interstate 405. Travel north on Highway 30 (also called St. Helens Road). Drive past the Burlington Northern/Southern Pacific rail yard and the intersection with NW Kittridge Avenue. Proceed through some gentle curves to a straight stretch of road, where you will see some homes and some commercial and industrial sites hugging the bottom of the forest. Midway through the straight stretch, just past the right-hand exit for NW Balboa Avenue, you will see the left-hand entrance to NW Saltzman Road. Take this small road to the park gate (0.7 mile) that marks the beginning of the hike.

TriMet: From downtown, take bus 16 (Front Avenue/St. Johns) or 17 (NW 21st Avenue/St. Helens Road). Disembark at St. Helens

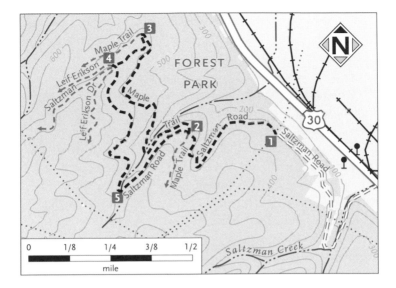

Road and NW 60th Avenue (bus stop 5363). Walk southeast 0.1 mile to Saltzman Road and proceed to the gate.

This short walk is perfect for a summer day, when the cool, deep forest is a welcome respite from the heat. The Lower Maple Trail boasts some beautiful big timber as well—a wonderful sight.

1 Saltzman is a broad, relatively smooth roadway ascending 407 feet in elevation from the gate to the point where it meets Leif Erikson Drive. This road is one of the four original routes across the Tualatin Mountains that allowed settlers to transport food from the fertile Tualatin Valley to their communities along the tidewater reaches of the Willamette River. Not surprisingly, the road was originally constructed by an early settler of the same name, and by 1889 it was designated as a county road. Today this access to the park is favored by runners, bicyclists, and walkers alike, though in lesser numbers than trails closer to downtown. The roadway is wide enough to accommodate them all.

During the late 1800s this area was the center of much of the logging activity that eventually stripped these slopes of their virgin old growth. In some areas huge stumps remain, giving mute testimony to the giants that towered over these hills. Most of these behemoths fell to stoke the settlers' fireplaces and steamship boilers, while others served as round timbers for building log cabins. It is still possible to spot evidence of the rough skidder tracks that were used in those early days to slide logs down the ravines to tidewater, where they could be collected into log rafts for easier transportation.

Streaked tricholoma (*Tricholoma portentosum*)

At the northern end of the park, logging of old growth continued into the mid-twentieth century. As recently as 1951, high-lead logging was used to extract large-scale timber from the park's steep slopes. This traditional logging method employs an elevated cable that is passed through a pulley atop a tall tree. As the cable is reeled in, the logs are dangled from the line so that only the bottom ends drag along the ground as they are pulled uphill to the collection point. The half-suspended logs are eventually deposited at the base of the elevated hoist, from whence they can be loaded onto a truck or railcar.

Even after the disappearance of most of the virgin timber in this area, the City of Portland continued to encourage more small-scale logging for firewood. In 1914 and again in 1937 the city operated a wood-cutting camp between Springville and Saltzman roads west of Leif Erikson to provide work for the unemployed and to supply fuel for impoverished families.

But logging was not the only reason why much of Forest Park was reduced to blackberry bushes by the 1950s. At least two catastrophic forest fires swept the park during those years. The first was the Bonny Slope fire of 1940 (described in the Fire Lane 3 and Upper Maple Trail Loop), which started in the vicinity of Fire Lane 2. Eleven years later, in August of 1951, the most devastating fire ever to affect Forest Park originated just north of Saltzman Road. Over three days it developed into a crown fire, sweeping across 25 percent of the park and burning more than 1200 acres. The fire was finally brought under control through a combined effort of the Portland, Multnomah County, and Washington County fire departments and the U.S. Forest Service. As with the Bonny Slope fire, Portland's lack of preparedness became an intense political issue.

And yet today our state of readiness is hardly assured. In 2005,

Portland State University graduate student David Kuhn published a report entitled "Development and Assessment of a Fire Model for Forest Park," an investigation into the likely consequences of a major forest fire. Combining data on historic weather patterns and detailed information about the current fuel load in the park, Kuhn simulated fires at six separate locations and demonstrated how the fires could leap into the lower branches of the conifers and thence climb into the treetops. Once a fire has reached the crown of a tree it can leap as far as half a mile downwind and start a new conflagration. The simulation showed that such a fire could easily sweep across Skyline Boulevard and inflict massive property loss upon the residents of Forest Heights.

Since the fire of 1951 the Saltzman Road and Springville Road portions of the park have recovered their stands of Douglas fir and western hemlock, which are now providing ample forest cover—especially in the steeper ravines, where the ample groves of maturing trees provide shade on a hot day.

2 Follow Saltzman Road up around a couple of bends, approximately a quarter of a mile, to where the Maple Trail descends to cross Saltzman as it turns sharply around another ridgeline. In the curve here the Maple Trail slips off the roadway on the right and descends into a steep canyon studded with beautiful, large Douglas firs. Any time of year this canyon of big timber exudes an aura of sylvan majesty, but during the hot summer months it can be especially refreshing as the cool atmosphere and shady slopes offer a welcome respite from the heat. And for any thirsty four-legged friends that may be accompanying you, there's a creek running along the bottom.

On the far side you will climb out of the canyon and pass into a mixed forest of Douglas fir, hemlock, and alder, dodging in and out of shallow ravines, whose creeks usually run dry in the summer.

In June and July you may spot the brilliantly colored red bane-berry (*Actaea rubra*) along this winding stretch of trail. Though unassuming, it is among the Northwest's most poisonous plants. Its sparse, crinkly leaves with saw-toothed edges often have one or two smaller alternate stem leaves. Overall the plant is stalky, with small white flowers and smooth, glossy, red or white ber-ries. As few as six berries can induce vomiting, bloody diarrhea, and finally respiratory paralysis. The common name derives from the Saxon *bana*, meaning "murderous." The Stl'atl'imx Indians' name for this plant originated from their word for "sick." They were said to chew the leaves and spit them on wounds.

3 Near the north end of the Maple Trail you will be traveling just above a large cliff that surrounds a narrow valley cut deep into the hillside. The floor of this narrow valley is the home of Port-land's car impoundment center and can be seen from Highway 30. Do not stray off this trail, as the cliff is at least 100 feet high. A chain-link fence runs along the top of the cliffs to prevent serious accidents.

As the trail crests the ridgeline, you will encounter a side trail that turns straight up the slope. The Maple Trail continues around the ridge before turning westward to join up with Leif Erikson Drive a mile or so further along. However, on this hike you will turn left at this intersection and climb the hill. This side trail immediately doubles back and runs southward just above the sec-tion of the Maple Trail you just traversed.

4 After 50 feet or so the trail turns westward and ascends the ridgeline until it emerges at the intersection of Saltzman Road

On a hot summer's day the cool, deep woods of Forest Park can bring relief, especially to those who insist on wearing a winter coat.

and Leif Erikson Drive. At this point you have climbed 407 feet from the gate to an elevation of 656 feet and have traveled about a mile.

This intersection is often busy with bicyclists resting, walkers choosing which route to take, and dog walkers trying to keep their hounds from getting tangled up with the others. A pile of lumber used for trail maintenance makes a nice spot to rest your legs.

5 The return trip down Saltzman Road is both shady and easy walking, with occasional glimpses of the Lower Maple Trail below. Another quarter of a mile finds you back at the gate.

(6) Ridge Trail Loop

TRAILHEAD NW Springville Road and Bridge Avenue
DISTANCE 3.5 miles round trip
DURATION Two hours and fifteen minutes
ELEVATION A total change of 1010 feet, with a low point of 235 feet and a high point of 1245 feet
CONDITIONS The Ridge Trail is new and well built, and NW Springville Road, though more than 165 years old, is graveled and well maintained.

FROM DOWNTOWN This hike begins 6.9 miles from West Burnside and Interstate 405. Driving north on Highway 30 (also called St. Helens Road), continue past NW Saltzman Road and beneath the St. Johns Bridge. Turn left at the traffic light immediately after the bridge. This puts you on NW Bridge Avenue (the access road to the bridge). After passing NW Germantown Road, turn right onto NW Springville Road and park anywhere along it. I usually park right down at the bottom.

TriMet: From downtown, take bus 17 (NW 21st Avenue/St. Helens Road). Disembark at Bridge Avenue and Springville Road (bus stop 599). You will alight from your bus at the trailhead.

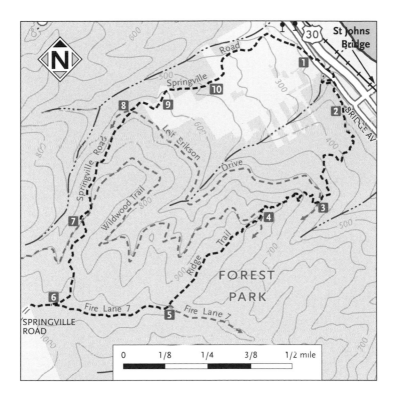

O n this excellent walk, lovely stands of mature Douglas fir
stretch from Highway 30 to the summit and back.

1 Although this trail can be accessed from the top of Springville
Road, off Skyline Boulevard, This hike begins at the intersection
of Springville and Bridge Avenue (the access road to the St. Johns
Bridge), immediately off Highway 30. Walk up Bridge Avenue,
crossing the bridge that is immediately south of the Springville
intersection. Just beyond the end of the bridge balustrade, a trail

From the bottom of Springville Road, turn
south to cross the bridge on Bridge Avenue.
Just beyond the end of the uphill balustrade a
trail leads back up into the woods, providing
convenient access to the Ridge Trail.

leads back into the woods providing a convenient shortcut to the Ridge Trail.

2 The official entrance to the Ridge Trail is located just south of where the St. Johns Bridge debouches on the western bank of the Willamette. A small set of stairs with signage to indicate the beginning of the trail leads up the reinforced embankment. This trail offers some fantastic views of the Willamette River and St. Johns Bridge

The bridge is named after the community of St. Johns, located across the river from our vantage point. The area was originally settled by the reclusive James Johns, who left Linnton in 1852 to pioneer Portland's northernmost ferry with a single rowboat.

With its graceful gothic arches, 400-foot-high towers, and 1207-foot main span, the St. Johns Bridge was and remains one of Oregon's architectural treasures. It was only through some very serious lobbying by the residents of St. Johns that this bridge was built in the first place. Penning verses and putting on vaudeville skits, the neighbors urged their Portland colleagues to replace the ferry with a bridge. "We've been patient and that you will allow," went a jingle, "but we're fed up with that ferry, and we want a bridge right now."

Contrary to popular legend, the St. Johns Bridge was not designed by Joseph Strauss, designer of the Golden Gate Bridge. It was designed by Holton Robinson and David Steinman, who celebrated their achievement by promptly flying a stunt plane over and under the bridge. Due to the bridge's proximity to the airport in Swan Island, some recommended painting it with yellow and black stripes to make it more visible to aircraft. However, the builders thumbed their noses at this garish suggestion and on St. Patrick's Day announced that the bridge would be painted a pale green to match the verdant hills that meet its western end.

Standing on that very slope, you will now turn your steps upward along the main trail. In a short distance you will enter a stand of tall Douglas firs. This lower part of the park is home to lots of wildlife, so keep your eyes open.

It's also a good place to find some interesting mushrooms. One of the most common is the orange milky cap (*Lactarius aurantiacus*). This bright orange mushroom can be found throughout the fall in Forest Park's conifer and mixed woods. The cap, which is 1–3 inches across, is rounded when dry but flat and viscid when wet. It's also identifiable by the fact that it bleeds a white milky substance when cut, hence the genus name.

Another easily recognizable mushroom occasionally found in Forest Park is fly agaric (*Amanita muscaria*). You will be familiar with it as the nasty poisonous mushroom from Disney movies— it has a bright red cap dotted with whitish spots. The common name refers to this mushroom's peculiar fascination to houseflies. Break up a fly agaric, place it in a shallow bowl with a bit of water, and flies will converge to drink the liquid. The effect is fatal, how-

Orange milky cap (*Lactarius aurantiacus*)

ever: they soon take off into a frenzied flight that ends in death. Death in humans is rare from fly agaric poisoning, but ingestion of this mushroom will certainly produce unpleasant side effects, including nausea, vomiting, and diarrhea.

About halfway up to Leif Erikson Drive you'll find a primitive bench located just off the trail for the quiet contemplation of the huge trees that surround you. Since this is a newer trail, you should find it in good shape and without too many visitors as it ascends to Leif Erikson Drive.

3 From Leif Erikson Drive the Ridge Trail ascends the ridge that carries Fire Lane 7 in a southeasterly direction into the park. Many trails descend from this ridge: Fire Lane 7a, the Hardesty Trail, the Ridge Trail, the Trillium Trail, and finally Springville Road. This hike takes you up the Ridge Trail.

4 The Ridge Trail crosses the Wildwood Trail at about 850 feet in elevation on its way to the crest of the ridge.

5 Once the Ridge Trail crests the promontory, it joins Fire Lane 7. Follow Fire Lane 7 back up the ridge and to the gate at the top of Springville Road.

Should you prefer to start this hike from the top, this is where you would begin. I recommend going down Springville Road and ascending by means of the Ridge Trail, as Springville Road is very steep and the Ridge Trail more lenient on the hamstrings.

6 Once you've reached the gate, turn right and follow Springville Road back down the wooded slope. The grade is quite steep, and the views through the woods can be lovely. Due to the graveled surface the going is rocky but not muddy—very helpful for this downhill trek.

As the population of Portland increases, so does competition for various recreational uses of Forest Park's trails, including this one.

7 Cross the Wildwood Trail a short way down the slope at an elevation of 990 feet.

8 At about 650 feet elevation you will cross Leif Erikson Drive. Just to the south of this intersection (on the uphill side of Leif Erikson) you might spot the ruined foundations of an old homestead. All around are groves of fruit trees that have been swallowed up in the encroaching forest. No doubt these fruit trees provided the ingredients for home-distilled spirits during Prohibition, as bootlegging was widespread throughout this area at that time.

9 Continue down Springville Road and after about a quarter of a mile you'll hit the final gate on the lower side. A private residence is located just beyond the gate, tucked into the woods to the south of Springville. It is fenced and clearly marked, but dogs might be attracted to the residents' chicken coop, so make sure to keep your beasts under control.

10 After another quarter of a mile you will reach the lower gate. It is usually open, although it warns drivers not to proceed beyond it. Below this is a small cluster of homes, a hidden community whose roots nearly predate the founding of Portland.

Springville Road was first built by the farmers and founders of the Springville community around 1846. Over the years the road's alignment often shifted, but Springville was considered to possess "the most even grade of any of the other four roads that lead from the Mountain down to the river road." By 1868 it had been surveyed and made into a county road. Today it remains an important fire lane and happens to be one of the most convenient ways to get to the center of the park quickly.

⑦ Willalatin Ridge Loop

TRAILHEAD NW Germantown Road near its intersection with Bridge Avenue

DISTANCE 6.1 miles round trip

DURATION Two hours and thirty minutes

ELEVATION A total change of 730 feet, with a low point of 260 feet and a high point of 990 feet

CONDITIONS This is a great trail for walking in the dry months, as both the Waterline and Wildwood trails can be muddy during the wet season. Both Springville Road and Leif Erikson Drive are well graveled. The lower portion of the Waterline Trail (below Leif Erikson) has some unimproved steep portions that offer less-than-adequate footing in wet weather. With good boots it's navigable, but slippery with shoes lacking adequate traction.

FROM DOWNTOWN This hike begins 7.2 miles from West Burnside and Interstate 405. Driving north on Highway 30 (also called St. Helens Road), continue past NW Saltzman Road and beneath the St. Johns Bridge. Turn left at the traffic light immediately after the bridge. This puts you on NW Bridge Avenue (the access road to the bridge). Take the first right, onto NW Germantown Road. Follow Germantown Road as it climbs the slope, about a third of

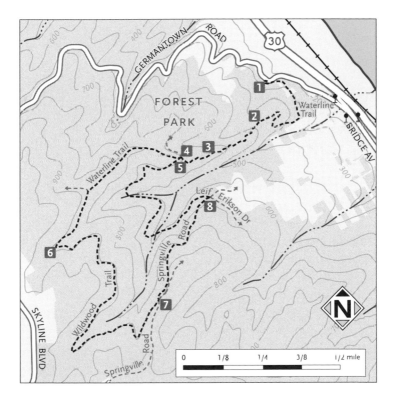

a mile. At this point the road takes a sharper left turn, then a right turn as it navigates in and out of a ravine. In the elbow of the turn you will see a small graveled area sufficient to hold two or three parked cars. Immediately beyond this you should note a steep, graveled road leading up into the forest. Park here and proceed up the road. (Note that further up Germantown Road there are more such elbow turns, with roads penetrating the forest, but they are clearly marked as private drives.)

TriMet: From downtown, take bus 17 (NW 21st Avenue/St. Helens Road). Disembark at the intersection of Bridge Avenue and Germantown Road (bus stop 597). Walk up Germantown Road 0.3 mile to the entrance of the Waterline Trail.

ALTERNATE ROUTE An alternate (and parallel) route into the park can be accessed by proceeding past NW Germantown Road on NW Bridge Avenue until you reach NW Springville Road (500 yards beyond Germantown Road). Turn right and ascend Springville (staying right) until it turns into a gravel road. It will pass through the small community of Springville, ascend behind the small homes, and pass through an open gate into a steep stretch that takes you directly into the park—all the way to the second and final gate. The second gate is located opposite the entrance of a private dwelling. By proceeding up Springville Road beyond the barrier (650 feet elevation) for 0.1 mile, you'll find yourself at the intersection with Leif Erikson Drive. From there you can follow the directions for this hike, beginning at waypoint 8 and proceeding northwest to the Willalatin Ridge. From there you will ascend the Waterline Trail to the Wildwood Trail and, turning south, complete the hike via Springville Road. Using this approach you will miss the lower portion of the Waterline Trail.

The Willalatin Ridge Loop features an unusual access route that takes you deep into the heart of Forest Park. Although you may encounter some traffic along the Wildwood Trail and Leif Erikson Drive, this seems a small price to pay for a walk through gorgeous stands of hemlock and cedar, with tall groves of Douglas fir in the deeper valleys and on the Willalatin Ridge.

1 This access route, referred to as the Waterline Trail, is little used and only partially improved. But in just 1.2 miles it pene-

Loki on the Wildwood Trail

trates the park and gets you up to Leif Erikson Drive without having to compete for parking or suffer through trailhead congestion at the Germantown access points to the Wildwood Trail and Leif Erikson.

2 The Waterline Trail begins as a fire lane broad enough to accommodate four-wheeled vehicles. It climbs upward, doubles back, and eventually emerges into a meadow at the top of the ridge.

As you pass through the meadow, be conscious that this kind of open, sun-drenched spot provides ideal growing conditions for poison oak (*Rhus diversiloba*). Although this dreaded plant is relatively rare in the mostly shady expanse of Forest Park, it may be lurking in more open areas.

Poison oak is a small, straggly shrub, typically only 2–3 feet high, with three-lobed, oaklike leaves. The foliage is often reddish and glossy as it first appears in spring but turns crimson by midsummer. The white berries (resembling the blisters they cause) emerge by late summer, though many plants fail to fruit at all. Poison oak is not common in the western valleys of Oregon, but it does occur, so knowledge of the plant and a bit of caution are in order.

Due to my habits of rummaging deep in the forest and frequently petting my dog, I contract blisters from this nefarious plant nearly every year. Typically I wash thoroughly with soaps designed to neutralize urushiol, the itch-producing oil found in poison oak, and apply a desiccant like calamine lotion or Tecnu scrub. The best advice I can offer is to wash your dog and your clothes, and above all else learn not to scratch the infected area. If you don't scratch the rash it will disappear within about a week, with the contagious and itchy period lasting only twenty-four to forty-eight hours.

3 At the far end of the meadow the road ends and a path continues upward along the spine of the ridge. This portion of the trail is unimproved and can prove treacherous in wet weather.

4 As you approach Leif Erikson Drive the trail levels out and weaves in and out of the cedars that help to keep this upper portion relatively dry. It emerges onto Leif Erikson as one of those semi-concealed paths that might be easily overlooked if you didn't know it was there. Needless to say this portion of the Waterline Trail is not identified with signage, so you should take note of where it emerges from the woods.

5 At Leif Erikson Drive proceed southward (turn left) and follow the roadway about 25 feet to where the upper portion of the Waterline Trail ascends. Here you will turn right to climb this more clearly marked trail as it ascends to the Wildwood Trail and eventually to Skyline Boulevard.

This portion of the Waterline climbs 0.3 mile from an elevation of 750 feet (at Leif Erikson Drive) to 860 feet (where it crosses the Wildwood Trail). The ascent is steep at first, but the trek is broken by two relatively level plateaus.

6 Upon reaching the Wildwood Trail, follow it southward (1.5 miles) until you reach Springville Road. On the way you'll penetrate deep into two draws as you wend your way to the next big ridge, along which Springville Road descends. As you hike deeper into these draws you'll find big stands of old Douglas fir as well as much hemlock and cedar. Unfortunately the trail can be pretty treacherous along this portion, so mud-resistant boots are in order during the rainy season.

If you know what to look for, you may spot some wild ginger (*Asarum caudatum*) growing along this trail. This evergreen perennial sports two dusky green, heart-shaped, 2- to 5-inch leaves on a long stalk. It is typically found in moist, shaded forests, often growing in large, ground-covering mats.

Boring plant, eh? Well, this humble plant has a long history. Although technically unrelated to the ginger plant, the ground-hugging wild ginger has a distinctive flavor and was used as a seasoning by trappers and pioneers. It is known to have antibiotic properties as well, and Pacific Northwest Indians used the roots in a tea for settling stomach pains. They also used its leaves as part of a preparation to combat tuberculosis, and some tribes even wore it as a good luck charm.

7 Turn left onto Springville Road (990 feet elevation). This road winds fairly steeply down the ridge, with wonderful views of stately Douglas firs to the left. Especially in deep winter, it's a treat to watch the mist and clouds swirl up through the giant tree trunks. Another 0.4 mile and you've reached the intersection with Leif Erikson Drive (700 feet elevation). At this point you may run into more pedestrian traffic coming from the Germantown Road access to Leif Erikson.

8 At the intersection of Springville Road and Leif Erikson Drive, turn left and follow Leif Erikson for 0.8 mile back to its intersection with the Waterline Trail—a mostly flat walk.

On the way keep an eye open for a tree on the right side of the trail that is riddled with woodpecker holes. Note how the holes are elongated vertically—the sign of a pileated woodpecker at work. (See pages 29–30 for more on this uncommon woodpecker.)

The most common woodpecker in our region is the northern flicker (*Colaptes auratus*), easily recognized by its brown-spotted wings, black-speckled breast, and black bib. The males have a distinctive red mustache, and both genders exhibit a telltale dipping motion when in flight. Flickers are extremely adaptable and have become an increasingly common part of our urban fauna. Listen for their distinctive cry of "kwik-wik-wik-wik."

The downhill portion of the Waterline Trail is hidden about 25 feet beyond where its upper portion intersects with Leif Erikson Drive, right in the bend of the road. The final descent to your car is only 1.2 miles. Be careful coming down this trail in wet weather.

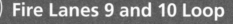

⑧ Fire Lanes 9 and 10 Loop

TRAILHEAD NW Germantown Road and Fire Lane 9, near the end of Leif Erikson Drive
DISTANCE 2 miles round trip
DURATION Two hours
ELEVATION A total change of 578 feet, with a low point of 90 feet and a high point of 668 feet
CONDITIONS This is fairly steep terrain, with a small portion of the hike traveling through Linnton and along Highway 30.

FROM DOWNTOWN This hike begins 8.5 miles from West Burnside and Interstate 405. Driving north on Highway 30 (also called St. Helens Road), continue past NW Saltzman Road and beneath the St. Johns Bridge. Turn left at the traffic light immediately after the bridge. This puts you on NW Bridge Avenue (the access road to the bridge). Take the first right, onto NW Germantown Road, and follow it to the northern terminus of Leif Erikson Drive and the associated parking area. Park alongside the cars on the south side of the road near the Leif Erikson trailhead or on the north shoulder of the road near the entrance to fire lanes 9 and 10.

TriMet: From downtown, take bus 17 (NW 21st Avenue/St. Helens Road). Disembark at the 9900 block of St. Helens Road (stop

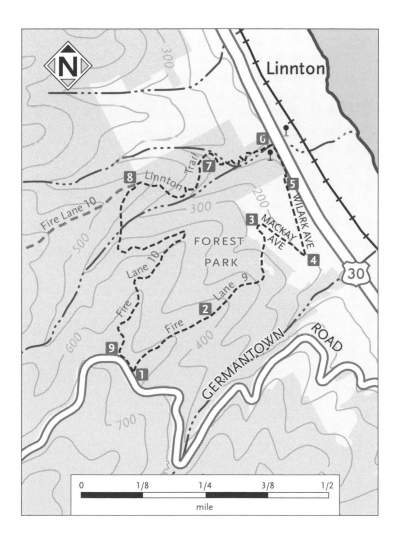

Linnton

Fire Lane 10

Linnton Trail

FOREST PARK

W ILARK AVE

MACKAY AVE

30

Fire Lane 10

Fire Lane 9

GERMANTOWN ROAD

Fire

| 0 | 1/8 | 1/4 | 3/8 | 1/2 |
mile

5354). This stop is located at the base of the hike. Proceed from waypoint 6 through to the end, and return on Fire Lane 9 using the directions given for waypoints 1–5.

This trail starts just opposite one of Forest Park's most popular hikes, and yet I rarely see anyone on it. Why? Because it's steep. I consider the grade well worth the trouble, however, since it assures that my walk is not constantly interrupted by convoys of runners for whom I must stand aside. Most importantly, this trail passes through some of the finest older-growth forest in the whole park.

1 If you parked near the terminus of Leif Erikson Drive, cross the road and locate the lower of two fire lanes that intersect with Germantown Road. The trailhead you're seeking is gated and marked as Fire Lane 9. Proceed on Fire Lane 9 straight down into the forest for a little more than half a mile. The trail quickly gets steeper—you will soon understand why it's preferable to descend rather than ascend it.

2 The higher portions of this descent run along a ridgeline that affords nice northward views across Linnton to the Willamette River.

Especially along the crest of this ridge, you will find that the trail is bordered by red alders (*Alnus rubra*) and big leaf maples (*Acer macrophyllum*). Fire Lane 9 is a prime area to see songbirds in the spring when they are feasting on the seeds and catkins produced by these trees. It is not uncommon to see western tanagers (*Piranga ludoviciana*), evening grosbeaks (*Coccothraustes vespertinus*), and warbling vireos (*Vireo gilvus*) all twittering away in the branches at once.

The Tualatin Mountains once supported gigantic trees, but double and even triple cutting have reduced most of the timber except in a few special groves.

Western tanagers are the most easily identifiable birds in the forest. The males can be recognized by their bright yellow body and red head, while the females are yellowish but lack the ostentatious red marking. They mostly subsist off insects but will welcome fruits and seeds in early summer. Flocks of western tanagers are often found in conifer forests, especially if the forest also includes some deciduous trees. Because these birds live in the upper canopy of the forest, the first clue to their presence is often their familiar call of "pid-a-dik" or "pad-ick."

Evening grosbeaks are unmistakable with their enormous heads and parrotlike bills. Flying in flocks, the males are black and yellow, while the females are a more muted gray-greenish yellow. They are noisy, like most herd-oriented creatures, and can be heard crying "pteer" as they fly overhead or devour seeds and fruits on the trees or off the ground. They are typically seen in spring and by summertime have migrated to the mountains, where they subsist off wild fruits.

3 As you descend further you will encounter a small stream and, near the bottom, a ruined water reservoir that once served the Linnton community. Just beyond, you will debouch onto MacKay Avenue, which you will follow down to Wilark Avenue.

4 Turn left onto Wilark and follow it to its end. Now you are walking through the Waldemere and Glen Harbor neighborhoods of Linnton.

Linnton is a feisty town that time has treated shabbily. It was founded in 1843 by entrepreneur Peter Burnett and General Morton McCarver, a veteran of the Indian Wars, at what they thought was the head of ship navigation on the Willamette River. The town was named after Senator Lewis Linn, who in 1843 initiated

the Oregon bill that provided land donations and grants to settlers. In *Recollections and Opinions of an Old Pioneer* (1880), Burnett
wrote of that time,

> We performed a considerable amount of labor there, most of
> which was expended in opening a wagon-road [Springville
> Road] thence to the Tualatin Plains, over a mountain, and
> through a dense forest of fir, cedar, maple, and other timber.
> When finished, the road was barely passable with wagons. Our
> town speculation was a small loss to us, the receipts from the
> sale of lots not being equal to the expenses.

In the 1890s Linnton saw the establishment of its first produc-
tion plant: a cannery that packed horse meat from eastern Oregon
for shipment to England. But dredging the Willamette soon established Portland as the area's center of commerce, and Linnton
became a gritty mill town whose surging population of immi-
grant workers labored at its many plywood mills. John Marinelli,
Linnton's longtime barber, described the town just after the turn
of the twentieth century: "The town was wild. There were several
saloons in it, men from the mills would come in and end up fight-
ing. You know we had our own jail, police and curfew!"

Portland annexed Linnton in 1915, but during Prohibition,
Linnton gained a new industry. As another longtime resident
reported, "There was nothing but bootlegging from here to St.
Helens. People had to try and keep from selling it to each other."
Many credit the tangle of hillside roads in Linnton as an inten-
tional defense against surprise raids by the police. Throughout
the area you can still find fruit trees deep in the forest—remnants
of moonshining.

As late as 1926, windjammers still called on Linnton's wharves
to pick up lumber destined for faraway Australia. But the rest

of the twentieth century brought Linnton little relief, beginning with the Depression, which cut deeply into employment at the mills. The cruelest blow came in the 1960s when the Oregon Department of Transportation decided to widen Highway 30. In so doing they wiped out half of Linnton's commercial establishments, leaving only the oldest buildings, including Linnton's famous Feed and Seed, which was originally built as a hotel in 1895.

In 2006, citywide industrial interests opposed a local effort to revitalize the area around the Linnton Plywood Mill and convert it into residential development. We haven't heard the last of Linnton, however: this scrappy little town seems to be set on continuing to press for a brighter future.

You can get a feeling for Linnton's struggles as you walk through its modest neighborhoods. Even nature has been hard on this community: deep ravines cut off one neighborhood from another, and Highway 30 and the railroad isolate these hillside homes from the riverfront.

5 At the northern end of Wilark Avenue, turn right and walk down the stairs to the sidewalk running along the west side of Highway 30. Turn left and walk to the Linnton bus turnout.

6 There you will find the Linnton Trail, which follows this deep ravine up to where it meets Fire Lane 10. Unfortunately, this part of the forest is choked with ivy, which has substantially diminished the quality of the wildlife habitat and even retarded the growth of new trees. Thankfully, increasing awareness of the problem is helping to allocate resources to combat the infestation. It will be a long struggle, but that's nothing new for Linnton.

7 As you ascend the many switchbacks of this steep trail, keep an eye open for the telltale soft reddish purple bark of the Pacific yew (*Taxus brevifolia*) growing among western hemlock and Douglas fir. This uncommon tree is much prized for the cancer-fighting chemical (taxol) found in its bark and needles.

If you think you hear an infant crying off to the right as you climb the 0.4 mile to Fire Lane 10, fear not it's the pygmy goats that belong to the farm on the next ridge to the north.

8 Upon reaching Fire Lane 10, turn left and follow it 0.6 mile to its junction with Germantown Road. As you stroll down and then up this last leg of the hike, take a moment to peer down the slope into the beautiful vistas of deeply forested hillsides and old Douglas firs growing alongside the trail. In summer this last segment of the walk is often cool and refreshing, especially in the late afternoon when the rest of Portland is baking.

9 Upon reaching Germantown Road you'll emerge about 100 feet above the entrance to Fire Lane 9, and below that is the parking lot for access to Leif Erikson Drive.

(9) Newton Road Loop

TRAILHEAD NW St. Helens Road and the BPA Road, just north of Marina Way

DISTANCE 4.4 miles round trip

DURATION Two hours and thirty minutes

ELEVATION A total change of 840 feet, with a low point of 60 feet and a high point of 900 feet

CONDITIONS The Newton Road Loop climbs upward through some of the wildest portions of Forest Park. It is a moderate to steep grade, but you will be well compensated by the savage beauty of the gorge from which Newton Road emerges. Lower Newton Road ascends a narrow valley alongside a relatively untrammeled creek that requires a couple of easy crossings. The Wildwood Trail is fairly level and not too muddy along this stretch, and the BPA Road is well graveled, making this hike ideal for inclement weather when other trails might turn into long, narrow bogs.

FROM DOWNTOWN This hike begins 8.8 miles from West Burnside and Interstate 405. Drive north on Highway 30 (also called St. Helens Road) to Linnton. As you leave Linnton's north end (just beyond the 55-mph sign) you'll see a set of high-power electric lines crossing high above the highway. At this point turn left into a very short dirt access road that marks the lower exit of the BPA

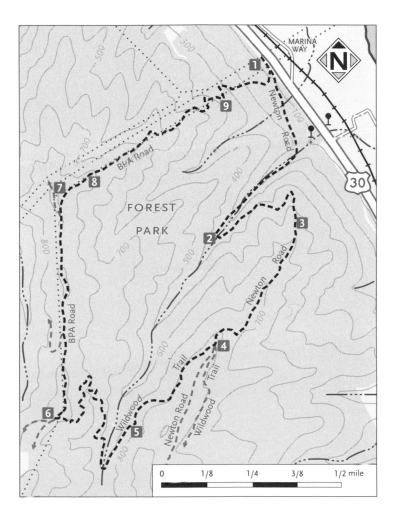

Road. The entrance to Newton Road is a narrow roadway carved into the hillside. The fire lane gate is only 25 feet from St. Helens Road. There is no sign to indicate that it is a trailhead. You can either park alongside St. Helens Road or squeeze your car along the upper verge of the roadway while still allowing the gate to be opened in case of an emergency.

TriMet: From downtown, take bus 17 (NW 21st Avenue/St. Helens Road). Disembark just north of Linnton at NW Marina Way and St. Helens Road (bus stop 10291). Walk north along St. Helens Road for 500 feet until you see the gate on the west side of the road.

I especially enjoy this hike during the hottest part of the summer, since the deep forest cover along much of the trail offers shade and cooler temperatures. In midwinter, when snow and ice are present, this remote corner of the park is resplendent with a rough, savage beauty. Lower Newton is a rugged old road that climbs upward from a wild streambed through one of Forest Park's oldest stands of Douglas fir. Via the Wildwood Trail it connects to the BPA (Bonneville Power Administration) Road, which offers a pastoral walk along a long, open ridge. At the promontory the trail offers panoramic views of the Cascades and the confluence of the Willamette and Columbia rivers.

1 Past the gate a very stony fire lane rises 50–75 feet in the next 50 yards. To the right the BPA Road proceeds uphill. Continue straight ahead on Newton Road as it ascends more gradually into a forested slope with a small pasture of mostly blackberries on the left. Skirt the brambles and proceed into a deep ravine with a wild creek that flows freely across the trail at more than one spot. If the water is running you'll be forced to jump across a few times—but nothing too difficult. No need to get your feet wet.

2 At the head of the ravine the path doubles back and begins to climb the southern face of the valley. Pace yourself: it's a long, steady climb from here. The road climbs upward along the southern face of the ravine into an old stand of woods dominated by Douglas fir.

The massive logging at the beginning of the twentieth century that reduced Forest Park to shrubs and bramble bushes has also made the park a perfect example of how forests evolve through successive stages of development—from tangled thickets, to shrubs, to mixed deciduous and conifer environments, and finally to older-growth stands. The lower reaches of Newton Road are a

The Willamette and Columbia rivers and
the Cascades as seen from the intersection
of Newton Road and the BPA Road

good model of a more mature forest, with large conifers approaching two hundred years in age. Near the BPA Road you will encounter forests in which conifers have not yet been able to displace the deciduous trees; red alder and big leaf maples still dominate the hillside. In the clear-cuts along the BPA Road you can also see the initial phases of thickets and shrubs.

As you climb out of the valley the road curves around, crosses a large fallen tree, and shortly thereafter begins to mount the eastern face of the Tualatin Mountains.

3 Shortly after making this turn and ascending steeply upward, you may notice a witness post survey marker that dates back to the 1854 survey conducted of the area. At the time of the original survey this part of the park was classified as "burned, second-rate timber." This may explain the presence of morels, which thrive on burned land.

While you're still climbing your way up Newton Road, keep an eye open for a yellow-tipped coral mushroom (*Ramaria rasilispora*). Otherwise known as the northwest spring coral mushroom, this fungus resembles broccoli in form but has a white base with yellow-tipped, branchlike structures that resemble coral. It can be seen in early spring.

Another popular mushroom often found on Newton Road (and throughout Forest Park) is the honey mushroom (*Armillaria mellea*), which grows on old stumps or logs or at the base of trees. This gilled mushroom grows in huge clusters and has both a ring and stringy white pith in the stalk. The cap is yellowish to brown with a smattering of darker hairs, often reminding me of mottled yellowish pig skin.

Newton Road continues uphill at a steady pace to where it crosses the Wildwood Trail.

4 Near the top of Newton Road, at an elevation of 810 feet, you will reach the Wildwood Trail. If you were to take the left-hand branch you would travel past the Newton Meadow and Fire Lane 10 to Germantown Road, some 1.7 miles due south. Proceeding further up the hill on Newton Road would quickly lead you over the top of a small rise and downhill directly to Newton Meadow, a small field that is accessible by car from Skyline Boulevard.

For this hike you will take the right-hand branch of the Wildwood Trail, which passes through some of the prettiest stands of old Douglas fir and cedar in the park. As a consequence of the many cedars found here, the Wildwood Trail is reasonably dry along this stretch. Given its distance from town, it is also relatively free of runners.

At one time the Wildwood Trail ended here, largely due to a 70-acre private in-holding, often referred to as Hole in the Park. A 1995 Metro bond measure to acquire open space helped the Friends of Forest Park to purchase this crucial parcel and thus extend the Wildwood to Newberry Road.

5 Although the Wildwood Trail initially turns west to head into the upper portion of a ravine, it eventually turns and traverses the northern slope of the valley. Then the trail doubles back, heading southwest, and ascends to 900 feet as it approaches the BPA Road. Look for patches of deciduous trees here: they signal unstable and rocky soil conditions.

This portion of the walk is noteworthy for its profusion of berries. During the summer and early fall months I rarely return without having gorged myself on at least three or four varieties of berries. Look for huckleberries along this path. They grow on bushlike shrubs and are typically the earliest berry for snacking, ripening in June and July.

This is also a favorite roosting ground for the bald eagles that commute to Sauvie Island each day to scoop walleyes (*Stizostedion vitreum vitreum*), smallmouth bass (*Micropterus dolomieu*), and common carp (*Cyprinus carpio*) from the river and from Sturgeon Lake. Listen for their deep-throated calls—most likely a complaint about your presence preventing them from flying up the valley to their roosts. Big birds cannot simply drop down into the forest canopy to reach their homes but must fly up the valley and approach their nests from below, hence their irritation with your intrusion.

6 After 1.15 miles on the Wildwood Trail you will emerge onto the BPA Road. Turn right to follow this pastoral road out to the point marked by the large overhead power lines. This is an exceptional road within the park because it is among the few trails not shaded by the forest canopy; rather, it runs along a cleared ridge at the end of which the BPA power lines cross. This portion of the walk always thrills me as I try to soak up the sunshine and look forward to the downhill portion of the trail yet to come.

7 The BPA Road climbs to 900 feet at the point where the road passes under the BPA power lines. Although this hike turns downhill immediately before the last rise under these pylons, take a moment to walk the few extra paces required to reach the promontory. The view from beneath the pylons is among the best in the park, providing a panorama of Sauvie Island and the confluence of the Willamette and Columbia rivers. Across the horizon you will see (from north to southeast) Mount Rainier, Mount St. Helens, Mount Adams, and Mount Hood. The channel below, once dominated by Multnomah Indians, now serves anglers catching smallmouth bass, walleyes, black crappie (*Pomoxis nigromaculatus*), white crappie (*P. annularis*), common carp, and the occasional Pacific lamprey (*Entosphenus tridentatus*) and white sturgeon

(*Acipenser transmontanus*). Three times a year runs of chinook salmon (*Oncorhynchus tshawytscha*), and twice a year runs of steelhead trout (*O. mykiss*), migrate up the lower Willamette, attracting flotillas of fishermen who span the river in "hoglines" of side-by-side fishing boats. Coho salmon (*O, kisutch*) and sockeye salmon (*O. nerka*) also migrate past the lower Willamette on their way to lay eggs at the base of the Willamette Falls.

8 Backtracking just about 50 feet you'll spot where the BPA Road actually bypasses the final knoll and begins its precipitous descent down the power-line clear-cut. This is my absolute favorite section of Forest Park, especially on a summer evening when I can watch the fishermen and boaters returning home up the river. In the distance you can see the big freighters coming up the river to the Port of Portland container terminals. Directly below, freighters load their cargoes and tugboats busily boss the big Japanese car transports into place. Way in the distance Mount St. Helens occasionally lets off a plume of steam as a reminder that all of this bucolic peace is very fragile.

9 Walking down is quite steep, and the lower portion of this road is very stony. A number of short tracks split off from the main road, but most of them peter out under the power lines. Take it slowly and walk on the grassy verge to avoid twisting an ankle. In the summer this path takes me forever to descend as I am forced to stop every two or three paces to sample the thimbleberries (July to early September), blackberries (August to October), wild raspberries (August), and ubiquitous salal berries (usually best late in the season, August to September).

Near the bottom you'll join up with Newton Road, and another 50 feet will bring you to the bottom gate. Be careful when backing out into traffic.

(10) Fire Lane 12 Loop

TRAILHEAD The end of NW Creston Road, off St. Helens Road
DISTANCE 2.8 miles round trip
DURATION One hour and forty minutes
ELEVATION A total change of 650 feet, with a low point of 250 feet and a high point of 900 feet
CONDITIONS This loop mostly consists of well-maintained fire lanes but also includes 0.25 mile of downhill bushwhacking through light undergrowth. It may be helpful to wear long pants and bring along some rose pruners.

FROM DOWNTOWN This hike begins 9.5 miles from West Burnside and Interstate 405. Driving north on Highway 30 (also called St. Helens Road), pass through Linnton and beneath some high-tension power lines. About a mile north of Linnton, take the exit for NW Harborton Drive on your left. This road twists to the left as it climbs the hill; follow it uphill until it levels out on NW Creston Road. Creston is about 200 yards long, with no parking at its far end, so park midway down the road on the shoulder and walk to the northwest end.

TriMet: From downtown, take bus 17 (NW 21st Avenue/St. Helens Road). Disembark just north of Linnton at Harborton Drive

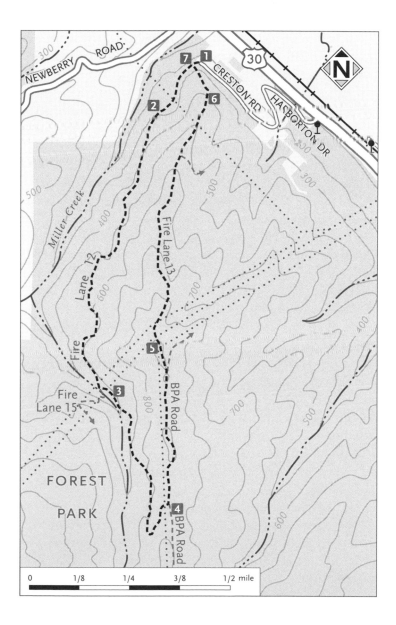

(stop 8744). Walk up Harborton (turning left at the first intersection) and continue uphill until you reach Creston Road. Proceed north on Creston to the gate at the end of the road.

This remote loop is undoubtedly among my favorite hikes in Forest Park. It encompasses some of the most scenic areas of the far northern end of the park, combining wooded hillsides with deep ravines, gurgling brooks, and open sunny vistas. It is an ideal hike for a clear day, as it provides spectacular views of Mount Rainer, Mount St. Helens, Mount Adams, Sauvie Island, and the confluence of the Willamette and Columbia rivers. The route features lovely, well-maintained trails through a pristine and remote little valley. There is nice, open walking along the BPA Road, with its stunning view from the promontory, and a seldom-used descent along Fire Lane 13. You are more likely to encounter deer on this hike than people. Please note, however, that about 100 yards of bushwhacking is required to return to the entry point.

1 At the end of Creston Road a forest gate marks the entry to Forest Park and Fire Lane 12.

2 Past the gate, Fire Lane 12 heads in a southwesterly direction and traverses the southern slope of the Miller Creek valley. This part of the trail accommodates bicycles, so you might encounter an occasional mountain biker whizzing down from Skyline Boulevard.

On the right the hillside drops off steeply. At the bottom of the ravine you may glimpse Miller Creek gurgling happily on its way to the Willamette River. The trail slope is moderately steep as you climb to an elevation of 875 feet where Fire Lane 12 intersects with the BPA Road. But it is not so steep as to demand chest-heaving exertion. Take it slow and steady so that you can enjoy the beauty of this remote valley with its overhanging cedars and plentiful deer. Halfway up the slope to the left of the trail you will find a seasonal pool (among the bushes) that is clearly popular with the wild residents of these parts.

Fire Lane 12 is an old road with a gravel base that keeps it reasonably dry in the wet season. As it winds along the hillside, note the hexagonal columns of basalt peeking out from under the trees. Sixteen million years ago, before the Cascade Range arose, flood basalts flowed like molten wax from eastern Oregon into the Portland area. Repeated floods of basalt continued to inundate the region, each layer eroded by time and reduced to clay. Then about eight million years ago tectonic forces pushed up the North Cascades and folded these basaltic flows in the Portland area to produce the very hills upon which

Yellow-tipped coral mushroom (*Ramaria rasilispora*), one of the many mushrooms found throughout this area

you are walking. The exposed basalt that can be seen below the tree roots of the overhanging cedars is all the evidence left of that mighty transformation.

3 As you ascend to the head of the Miller Creek valley (about 650 feet elevation) you'll reach a three-way intersection. Straight ahead is Fire Lane 15, which continues up the valley a bit further. Across the creek you might also spot the remnants of Fire Lane 14, which traverses the opposing flank only to end abruptly, presumably at the end of the park property. Take the left-hand alternative and climb the southern flank of Miller Creek valley on Fire Lane 12. This short ascent to the BPA Road is the steepest portion of the trail, so pace yourself.

4 Fire Lane 12 intersects the BPA Road about halfway between its start at Skyline Boulevard and the scenic promontory at the high point of the ridge. At this intersection turn left and follow the BPA Road northward along the ridge to the promontory, where you will undoubtedly enjoy the terrific view.

Just prior to reaching the promontory you'll see one spur of the road branch off to the right and head down the hill under the power lines. This is the continuation of the BPA Road, which ends at Highway 30. (See the Newton Road Loop for an exploration of this track.)

5 Stay left to ascend the small hillock under the power lines. Take a moment to rest here and feast your eyes on a magnificent view of Sauvie Island and the confluence of the Willamette and Columbia rivers.

Across the Willamette you will see the Port of Portland's Rivergate Industrial District, with its container terminal facing the

Columbia River and heavy industrial operations such as Schnitzer Steel and Columbia Grain facing the lower Willamette.

Had you stood here two hundred years ago you would have looked down directly upon the thriving villages of the Multnomah Indians, who built sturdy lodges colorfully decorated with carved totemic images along the shores of Sauvie Island. Rows of brightly colored canoes with carved figures on the prow and stern marked the locations of several villages. The men, wearing mountain-beaver robes and conical hats, built fires and prepared meals in this area. The women wore shorter robes and skirts fashioned out of shredded cedar bark. The very old and young bustled along the shores, tending to the fish traps. Life was good for the Multnomah, blessed as they were with a plethora of trout, salmon, sturgeon, elk, deer, wappato, camas lily, salal berries, and even tobacco.

Meriwether Lewis estimated the Multnomah Indian population at around eight hundred. After the establishment of Fort Vancouver in 1824, delegations of them visited the fort daily, but in 1829 they suddenly ceased coming. When people were sent to investigate, they found the villages littered with hundreds of dead bodies. Measles and malaria had extinguished the Multnomah in a matter of weeks.

In their legends the Multnomah told of a great canoe with white wings that would ascend the Columbia. It was said that when it came to rest in the evening it would issue forth a cloud that produced a great roar, and that the cloud would strike terror into the heart of all who heard and saw it. From the sides of the vessel would come black clouds, and wherever these noxious fumes alighted they would bring death and utter destruction. And so it occurred.

Beyond the promontory you'll see that the track continues

down to a second set of power lines and then veers to the right. This is Fire Lane 13, which descends to a lower set of power lines strung along the hillside at an altitude of about 500 feet. Follow Fire Lane 13.

Leaving the ridgetop, you now descend through a very pleasant forested ridgeline. Halfway down, a short spur heads off to the right, but ignore the temptation to explore that road: it serves only as an access road to another set of power poles located at the end of an adjoining ridgeline.

Fire Lane 13 terminates on a small promontory with a nice view to the northwest across Newberry Road toward the Tualatin Mountains and the Sauvie Island Bridge. In the summer the power poles on this knoll are a favorite roost of the turkey vultures (*Cathartes aura*) that migrate north from California to patrol these slopes each summer.

6 Now here's the tricky part! Continue straight across the promontory, passing to the right of the power poles, and push on through the thick vegetation on the far side of the clearing. If you look carefully you will see where the deer have forced a passage through the vegetation. Take advantage of their efforts and you'll emerge in a medium-dense forest that slopes steeply downward directly ahead.

Turn left, facing northward, and follow the ridgeline down; you'll come out above the entrance to Fire Lane 12 about 100 yards down the slope. Although there is no real path through this section of the woods, it's pretty easy to stay on track by simply descending along the top of this northerly ridgeline. Eventually you'll see the roofs of the houses below on Creston Road to the right. Don't be tempted to descend directly toward them—that's a very steep slope. Keep to the ridgeline and carefully descend in a northerly direction among the ferns and bushes. Fire Lane 12 has a 5- to 6-foot shoulder on the uphill side, so the road will not be visible until you are directly at the shoulder. I typically try to descend the shoulder using one of the deer tracks; otherwise I descend alongside one of the bigger trees, using it as something to hang on to as I slide down the final few feet to the roadway.

7 Once on the roadway you should see the gate at the entrance to Fire Lane 12 just to the left, or eastward of the ridgeline you descended

(11) Fire Lane 15 Loop

TRAILHEAD NW Skyline Boulevard and Fire Lane 15

DISTANCE 2.8 miles round trip

DURATION Two hours

ELEVATION A total change of 250 feet, with a low point of 750 feet and a high point of 1000 feet

CONDITIONS Fire Lane 15, Fire Lane 12, and the BPA Road are well graveled, but the Wildwood Trail is pretty muddy along this stretch.

FROM DOWNTOWN This hike begins 10.5 miles from West Burnside and Interstate 405. Driving north on Highway 30 (also called St. Helens Road), continue past NW Saltzman Road and beneath the St. Johns Bridge. Turn left at the traffic light immediately after the bridge. This puts you on NW Bridge Avenue (the access road to the bridge). Take the first right, onto NW Germantown Road. Drive up Germantown Road to NW Skyline Boulevard. Turn right on Skyline Boulevard and proceed northward for 1.6 miles, passing under the BPA high-power electric lines, until you come to an open area with modern housing developments on both sides of the road. On the right you will see a trail starting behind a barrier. Overhead another set of power lines marches down the Miller Creek valley. Park near the entrance on the right side of the road.

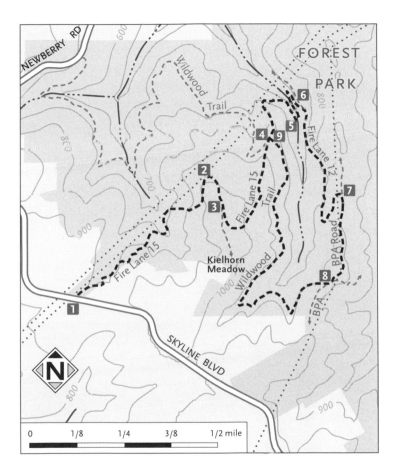

Winding its way along the extreme northern edge of Forest Park, this hike includes nice open vistas on both Fire Lane 15 and the BPA Road. The section of the Wildwood Trail on this loop features nice footbridges in a thick, middle-aged mixed-conifer forest.

1 Beyond the gate the well-maintained Fire Lane 15 skirts the southern edge of the power-line clear-cut, dipping in and out of the side ravines. Starting at Skyline Boulevard at an altitude of approximately 900 feet, the trail dips to 800 feet before rising to nearly 1000 feet at the promontory, about half a mile from the gate.

2 This point affords a great view north toward Sauvie Island, Mount St. Helens, and Mount Rainier. To the east you'll see another ridge across which power lines are slung like giant clotheslines. This is actually the promontory at the end of the BPA Road, a popular destination because of its spectacular view of the Columbia River and Sauvie Island.

The hike now takes you southward. Turning to the right, head back into the forest and past another forest gate.

Honey mushroom (*Armillaria mellea*)

3 Immediately after the gate you will encounter a spur track that heads upward to the right. This short woodland lane leads to the Kielhorn Meadow, which was purchased and donated by the Friends of Forest Park in the 1980s to preserve this precious woodland glade. It is a lovely spot for a secluded picnic. Conveniently enough, it can also be accessed from Skyline Boulevard just to the south of where you parked. However, on this hike you will continue downhill along the main track.

4 As you proceed past the Kielhorn Meadow's spur, the trail begins to drop down, and 0.4 mile beyond the gate you just passed you will arrive at the intersection with the Wildwood Trail. In all you've covered a mile since beginning the hike.

5 Continue down Fire Lane 15, which drops to the bottom of the ravine (750 feet elevation) in 0.3 mile. This is a steep route and best done walking downhill. At the bottom, Fire Lane 15 drops to the back of a narrow ravine before crossing a small stream and then heading north for a short distance to intersect with Fire Lane 12.

6 You've now walked the full length of Fire Lane 15: 1.35 miles. From here you will ascend Fire Lane 12 for half a mile to the BPA Road, which runs the length of the next ridge—about 100 feet in elevation above your current position. The lower portion of this ascent is steep, so pace yourself.

7 Half a mile later and a hundred feet higher you emerge from the forest into a clear-cut corridor that runs along the full length of the BPA power-line ridge. This promontory and the road leading up to it afford great views if the weather gods should smile upon you and provide sunshine and clear vistas. It has attracted growing numbers of walkers as the population in Portland has increased. It remains among my favorite haunts, but these days I try to access it via more remote trails so as to avoid most of the foot traffic. Aside from this hike, both the Fire Lane 12 Loop and the Newton Road Loop use the BPA Road for part of the journey.

At the junction of Fire Lane 12 and the BPA Road turn right, toward the intersection with the Wildwood Trail, 0.3 mile ahead. Behind you the BPA Road curves northward until it crests the promontory, upon which the massive high-tension power pylons stand, and from which point you can enjoy a spectacular view to the north. If you're inclined and time permits, it's worth the forty-five-minute detour to the promontory and back.

8 At the intersection of the BPA Road and the northbound portion of the Wildwood Trail (you will already have passed the southbound junction) turn right onto the trail and proceed to the west. Most of this portion of the Wildwood traverses a middle-aged mixed-conifer forest consisting of thicker stands of hemlock, cedar, and Douglas fir, and some thinner stands of alder. The Wildwood Trail can get pretty muddy along this 0.9-mile stretch to where it intersects with Fire Lane 15, and it does experience moderate traffic (mostly from people accessing the trail via Newberry Road). But the trail also features some lovely footbridges as it winds in and out of the various draws.

9 After you return to the intersection of the Wildwood Trail and Fire Lane 15, proceed steeply uphill, climbing to 100 feet in elevation in the next quarter mile. After this point the fire lane levels off to a more gradual climb, past the Kielhorn Meadow (above the trail) and back to the viewpoint.

Another half mile along the power-line clear-cut brings you back to Skyline Boulevard.

Northern Tualatin Mountains

Following cougar tracks after snowfall. Cougars do live in these forests, even as close in as NW Cornell Road, but are seldom seen and have never been known to attack people in this region.

(12) Ennis Creek Hike

TRAILHEAD NW Newberry Road, 0.7 mile off St. Helens Road
DISTANCE 1.4 miles one way, 2.8 miles round trip
DURATION One hour and thirty minutes
ELEVATION A total change of 560 feet, with a low point of 317 feet and a high point of 877 feet
CONDITIONS An infrequently used logging road rises almost 500 feet as it steadily ascends a ridge north of Ennis Creek. Beyond the crest of the hill, the route of this hike proceeds along a lightly used and occasionally overgrown path. I recommend wearing long pants and, if you plan to explore the side trails, bringing rose pruners to get through any difficult patches of brambles.

FROM DOWNTOWN This hike begins 10.2 miles from West Burnside and Interstate 405. Drive north on Highway 30 (also called St. Helens Road). About an eighth of a mile past Linnton, turn left up NW Newberry Road. After following the hill for 0.7 mile, a dirt road leads off the right shoulder to a locked forestry gate. Park nearby.

TriMet: From downtown, take bus 17 (NW 21st Avenue/St. Helens Road). Disembark at the intersection of St. Helens Road and NW Riverview Drive (bus stop 11016). Walk south along St. Hel-

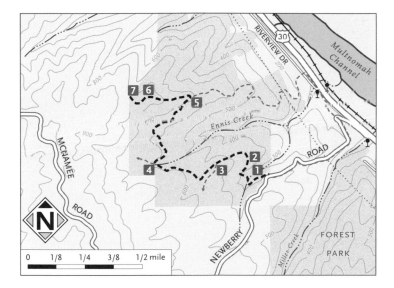

ens Road until you reach Newberry Road. Follow this road to the gate.

This delightful hillside ramble winds along a wide, trimmed track through a very young conifer forest. Most of the trails that crisscross these densely overgrown slopes around the Ennis Creek watershed lead nowhere in particular, but the lovely vistas and pastoral lanes that get you there are well worth exploring. And somewhere beyond the end of this trail is the lost Phillips Cemetery.

1 Begin this hike by dropping off the shoulder of Newberry Road (elevation 407 feet) and skirting the gate. The trail proceeds downhill a short distance before beginning its long, gradual ascent.

2 A third of a mile onward you will encounter your first side trail, which branches off to the right at an elevation of 467 feet. This side trail is relatively short and terminates in a wall of blackberries at the end of a short ridge.

3 Another trail branches off to the left roughly half a mile into the hike. This trail is more substantial and worth exploring, but also leads nowhere.

Most managed forestlands at this stage of their regrowth are thinned, meaning they are cleared of underbrush and faster-growing deciduous trees. This weeding process allows a dense conifer forest to take hold in much less time. Without the thick underbrush, the forest develops a more accessible understory that sustains a larger population of animals; it is also able to retain more water stored in the moss and moist soils. The Ennis Creek watershed is a good example of how the lack of forest management undermines the development of an effective habitat—at least until natural succession eventually allows the conifers to crowd out the vines, brambles, and deciduous trees. From a hiker's perspective this means it's impossible to bushwhack through these very dense stands. And believe me, because I've tried many times and have had to relent, finding the undergrowth too thick to penetrate.

4 Another 0.3 mile onward you cross Ennis Creek itself, a small, unimpressive trickle that disappears into the thick undergrowth. Just beyond the creek another spur leads off on the left-hand side of the trail. Ignore this side trail and continue upward to the right, ascending from an elevation of 604 feet to the top of the first ridge at 738 feet.

5 At the top of the ridge the track emerges, affording a view to the south of the thick tangle of young forest through which you have

Use the gated entrance downhill from
this view of the Ennis Creek watershed.   **117**

climbed, and beyond that the northern end of Forest Park. From this vantage point the Willamette River is visible, as are the power lines that cross the bottom of this property. Below the power lines a gravel service road runs northward to the Angell Quarry. However, you cannot use this road to access Metro's Burlington Creek property, since transit through the quarry is expressly prohibited.

It is possible to execute a looped trail if you continue past the crest of the hill and descend eastward down the side trail that leads toward the power lines. To make the loop, follow the trail down to where it ends just 50 feet above the actual power-line towers. From there follow the rudimentary track that continues downward and passes directly under the tower itself. The service road is located immediately beyond the tower, about 10 feet below its base. Turn right on the road and follow it down as it passes between two houses and onto a road that leads down to Highway 30. Head right (south) along Highway 30 to the intersection with Newberry Road and follow Newberry Road back to the gate.

To complete the Ennis Creek Hike, ignore this alternate route. Upon reaching the crest of the hill turn left at this hilltop clearing and walk northward into a small opening in the woods. Upon entering this glade you should see a rough trail heading up a long ridgeline to the left. Follow this narrow path, which is covered in deep grasses and crowded on both sides with bushes and blackberries. Continue upward for 0.2 mile. On the way you will pass by a white survey marker to your right.

6 Just beyond the white marker the narrow path leads into a broader track. This old road also descends the ridgeline and crosses your path before dropping down the northern flank of the ridge. Turn uphill (left) onto this track and continue to climb the ridgeline. You have now ascended to an elevation of 874 feet and have covered 1.3 miles from the gate.

7 Only 0.1 mile up the ridge the track emerges into a grassy clearing that marks the top of the second ridge (elevation 877 feet). As you enter the clearing from its southeast corner, you will observe that a well-maintained, grassy road passes through it, entering from the upper southwest corner and heading downhill in a southerly direction. This road marks the corner of private property belonging to a house situated at the very top of the hill. A number of old logging roads diverge from this clearing, but in the interest of avoiding the possibility of trespassing on the private property associated with the houses on the ridge above, the hike ends in this idyllic pasture.

Perhaps some day Forest Park will be extended to this point and beyond. In the 1980s the Friends of Forest Park negotiated an easement that would allow hikers to trek from the Ennis Creek property across this nearly impenetrable slope to Metro's Burlington Creek property on the far side of the quarry. This is not currently a legally accessible route, however, and the extreme density and steepness of these slopes make any penetration all but impossible.

Somewhere in this area is the long-lost Phillips Cemetery. I have searched these steep hillsides for signs of this pioneer cemetery, but alas, the ravages of shifting soils, dense undergrowth, and wicked bramble patches seem to have obliterated all signs of it.

At this point the hike has reached its conclusion, and I recommend you return by the same path you entered. With the exception of the trail described at waypoint 5, which returns you to the start via Highway 30 and Newberry Road, you will find that returning along the original track is the best option. While many of the side trails are picturesque and remote, none of them connect with Newberry Road or the Wildwood Trail.

(13) Burlington Creek Loop

TRAILHEAD NW McNamee Road, 0.3 mile off St. Helens Road

DISTANCE 3.2 miles round trip

DURATION Two hours and thirty minutes

ELEVATION A total change of 450 feet, with a low point of 150 feet and a high point of 600 feet

CONDITIONS This logging road is wide, well maintained, and reasonably level, making for a fairly undemanding and relatively dry walk.

FROM DOWNTOWN This hike begins 12.9 miles from West Burnside and Interstate 405. Drive north on Highway 30 (also called St. Helens Road). Pass through Linnton and the hamlet of Burlington, about 10 miles from downtown Portland. After passing through Burlington you will approach a traffic light that marks the intersection with Cornelius Pass Road. About 100 yards before this intersection, a road bends up the slope to the left: that's NW McNamee Road. Follow this road for 0.3 mile, passing under a railroad trestle and around a couple of sharp turns. Turn into the first side road branching off to the left, and park near the gate. This is the entrance to the Burlington Creek watershed.

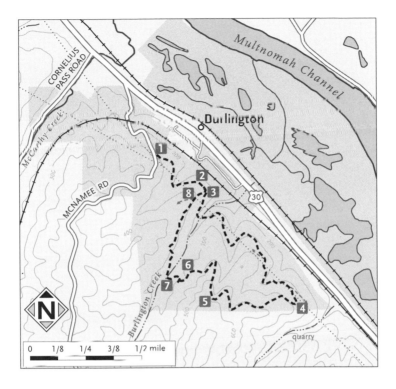

This lovely walk includes open vistas along a logging road that traverses the eastern face of the Tualatin Mountains. There are many hawks and eagles in the area, and I've occasionally encountered deer and coyotes. This is one of the best close-in, lesser-known trails in these mountains. The Burlington Creek property was purchased in 2000 by Metro and may eventually be linked with the Ennis Creek property to enable a major extension to Forest Park.

1 The gate is at an elevation of about 300 feet, and the road dips to about 200 feet in the first draw you cross.

As you hike this trail you may notice some unusual wildlife along its shoulders. I was fortunate enough to find a praying mantis (*Mantid religiosa*) here once, although these creatures are not commonly seen in this region. Also look for Oregon Iris (*Iris tenax*) blooming by the wayside.

2 Just past the first ravine, 0.3 mile into the hike, you may notice a side trail on the left. This footpath descends to the railroad tracks that run along the base of the property. From there the path connects to a cluster of homes above Burlington.

There is a house in Burlington . . .

As you drove by Burlington on your way to McNamee Road, you will have undoubtedly spotted the towering five-story hulk looming on the uphill side of the community. This gothic monstrosity is said to have been a bordello that saw its heyday during the 1920s, when the road to St. Helens was infamous for its iniquitous watering holes. Those who have taken the time to explore the relic report that it houses a beautiful if somewhat dilapidated antique bar and is swarming with bats amidst a jumble of moldering detritus. (I don't recommend a closer look at this testament to ruination.)

3 The road forks beyond the next bend, 0.4 mile into the hike. The right-hand road climbs the slope to traverse the hillside at a higher elevation, eventually winding its way to the back of the gulley where a tall stand of old trees is clearly visible from a distance. This is the road that you will use on your return trip. The left-hand

Progressive timber management practices routinely call for preserving large trees that house the eyries (nests) of bald eagles. This stately fir tree dominates the previously logged slopes but is itself dwarfed by the old-growth trees towering behind the photographer.

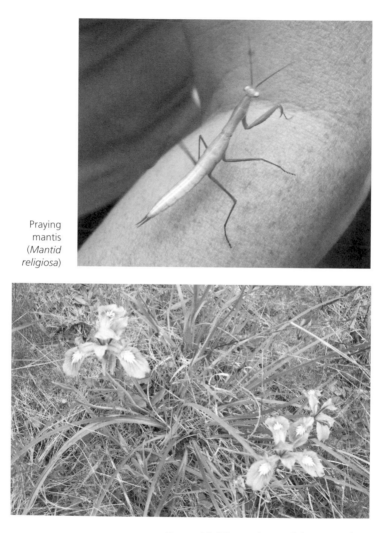

Praying
mantis
(*Mantid
religiosa*)

Oregon iris (*Iris tenax*), one of the many unique
wildflowers found throughout this area

option continues southward, traversing the slope at a lower elevation. Take this lower road, which dips down to 150 feet in the next draw and then climbs to follow the contour of the hill at about 350 feet for another mile.

4 At the southeastern end of the Burlington Creek property, 1.5 miles into the hike, the logging road splits, with a lower trail continuing south toward the Angell Quarry. I don't recommend following that track, as trespassing in the quarry is strictly forbidden. Take the upper track instead, which loops back and gradually ascends the slope.

5 In 0.2 mile the trail reaches its summit at about 600 feet before dropping down the slope again. As you descend along the ridgeline, take note of the broken-top old-growth Douglas fir dominating the slope on the left; it's often been used as an eyrie (nest) by the bald eagles that frequent the area.

You are likely to find bracken ferns growing in the open spaces along the edge of the track here. This prolific fern grows in meadows and clearings as well as on sterile sandy soils. It can be found in burns, avalanche tracks, and even around acidic lakeshores and bogs. The rhizomes actually sink into the soil to a depth that allows the fern to withstand forest fires and flourish after the fire has burned out. Indians traditionally chewed the fibrous stems and dried the mulch for tinder. Most Northwest tribes harvested bracken in late summer, cooking them in traditional pit ovens and serving them with fish eggs or oil. (Neither treatment, I suspect, will hold much appeal for contemporary gourmets.)

After passing the eyrie, the trail along the ridgeline doubles back toward the left. Here it begins to traverse the northern slope of the ridge you've just descended. The broken-top Douglas fir will be directly above you.

6 As you approach the bottom of the slope a massive stand of old-growth Douglas firs will become visible at the head of the ravine. In the 1980s I worked with the Friends of Forest Park to help purchase a 38-acre parcel including a 20-acre stand of unique ancient trees. This stand was later added to the surrounding 332 acres of the Burlington Creek watershed woodlands purchased by Metro. In 2001 eagle activity was detected in the old-growth grove, including the fledging of young bald eagles. As a result the Friends of Forest Park adopted a management plan for the area that limited access to guided visitations during specified times of the year. A small trail through the grove was inaugurated in 2005; you will spot the upper entrance emerging from the grove on the left. This low-impact trail is clearly a labor of love, with hand-carved bridges and steps that guide visitors carefully along the fragile forest floor. Since access to this special protected grove is restricted, please contact the Friends of Forest Park to make arrangements for a visit.

7 After bypassing this ancient stand of 400-year-old trees, continue down the trail that skirts the edge of it. At the base of the slope where the trail crosses Burlington Creek, you will see a large wooden sign that commemorates the donors who made acquisition of the old-growth grove possible. This is 2.4 miles into the hike. From here the trail leads gently uphill.

You may spot the white, lilaclike flower clusters of oceanspray (*Holodiscus discolor*) hanging over the road. Later in the season the clusters turn brown, but they stay on the bush through the winter. This shrub is also known as creambush and, because of the extreme hardness of its wood, ironwood. The wood can be made even harder by heating it over a fire. Before the introduction of nails, ironwood pegs were used in carpentry. Northwest Indians traditionally used it to make scrapers, hooks, and barbecuing sticks, and more recently knitting needles.

8 Less than half a mile onward, or 2.8 miles into the hike, you will finally reach the intersection with the main trail that was used to enter the area. Now turn left and retrace your steps back to McNamee Road, another 0.4 mile to the north.

(14) McCarthy Creek Loop

TRAILHEAD Across the street from 11323 NW Skyline Boulevard

DISTANCE 2 miles round trip

DURATION Forty-five minutes

ELEVATION A total change of 225 feet, with a low point of 630 feet and a high point of 855 feet

CONDITIONS This graveled logging road is well maintained.

FROM DOWNTOWN This hike begins 11.8 miles from West Burnside and Interstate 405. Drive north on Highway 30 (also called St. Helens Road). About an eighth of a mile past Linnton, turn left (west) up NW Newberry Road. Turn right onto NW Skyline Boulevard. You'll find the gate to the logging road just past the intersection of Skyline and NW McNamee Road. Park in front of the gate, but do not block access. Please note that since this is privately held timberland it is particularly important to make as little impact as possible here. Remain on the logging road to avoid trespassing.

This is a nice short hike, mostly level and with all-weather roads, ideal for less intrepid woodsmen or for those traveling with kids. It affords beautiful views of Cornelius Pass and the

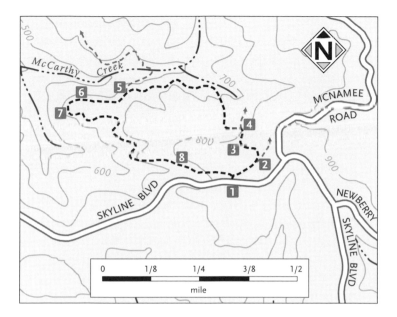

Tualatin Mountains stretching away endlessly to the north—a great introduction to what lies in store for the more ambitious hikes in this series. Elk are known to frequent the area described in this hike.

1 The trail immediately splits, heading both left and right. Take the right-hand spur—uphill. This will wind through a grove of young fir trees curving to the left (westward).

2 Ignore the short trail that branches off to the right; it connects with McNamee Road (0.2 mile). As the path proceeds gently downhill, you will enter an open glade planted with seedlings.

3 The glade faces a small hillock that was logged not long ago and is now slowly being reforested by young firs that stretch up the hillside. In the foreground you'll see lots of bright yellow Scotch broom (*Cytisus scoparius*), an invasive weed that has overrun most of the coastal areas from California to British Columbia.

4 In this clearing you'll come to an intersection (0.9 mile from the gate). The right-hand trail winds around the upper reaches of the basin for about a third of a mile, concluding in a dead end on the opposing slope.

Take some time here to examine the ground for animal tracks. One of the best ways to learn about the activities of the animals in an area is to learn to identify their tracks, their idiosyncratic ways of marking their territory, and their scat. (*Scat*, of course, is the polite word for animal doo-doo.) It's also a very effective way to determine who's been hanging out on your trail.

In Forest Park and even more so beyond the park, you're likely to see plentiful signs of both black-tailed deer and elk. The black-tailed deer live in small family groups, feeding primarily on salal, huckleberries, blackberries, and thimbleberries. Their tracks are heart-shaped (1.25–3.5 inches across) with the bottom end of the heart pointing in the direction of the deer's direction of travel. The tracks left by the hind feet often cover those made by the front feet, and the front hoof is frequently splayed to allow the deer better traction.

Deer scat is pellet-shaped (0.5 inch in diameter) and usually deposited in small heaps. When fresh it has a wet, shiny appearance, turning dull in a day or so and eventually becoming paler. In winter the scat will be more distinctly pellet-shaped, but as the moisture content of the food increases they tend to bunch into larger clumps.

Elk tracks are both larger (3–4.5 inches across) and rounder than those of black-tailed deer. As with deer, the gait of an elk is an alternating, double-registering pattern with the hind hoof obliterating the front track. But elk are herd animals, like cows, moving in groups and leaving very noticeable trails.

Elk scat pellets are slightly elongated and bell-shaped with little points at the top of the bell. In the summer months when the feed is moister, they tend to clump together to form flat chips or even plops 5–6 inches in diameter.

Take the left-hand trail and proceed downhill past the young seedling fir trees. Look for deer and elk scat: it abounds in this area.

5 Another 0.3 mile will take you to the north side of the hillock to where the trail intersects with another lower logging road. This logging road (to the right) drops down into the valley, crosses the headwaters of McCarthy Creek, and continues across a more recent clear-cut. Eventually it splits into two trails. The upper spur turns back and recrosses the clear-cut higher on the slope before petering out in the bushes. The lower trail continues northward but also splits into two distinct tracks. The upper of these two spurs connects to Pauly Road via a short trail that intersects the trail in the final bend of this track.

6 For the purposes of this hike, ignore this northerly detour and proceed along the back of the hill (turn left). You will be rewarded with a lovely view westward across the McCarthy Creek basin, over Cornelius Pass Road, and into the Tualatin Mountains as they extend toward the coast.

7 Another tenth of a mile will take you out on the ridge and around the point. A shortcut runs just behind the point, if you're willing to miss the view.

Along the way, or wherever you notice disturbed ground in the Tualatin Mountains, you may run into the notorious stinging nettle (*Urtica dioica*). Its narrow leaves are shaped like a mint leaf with a saw-toothed edge, and small flowers hang off the stem in drooping clusters. The leaves are covered with tiny hairs whose brittle ends break off to release formic acid, which causes a rash and itches for up to a few hours. Even dogs can be bothered by this plant and will develop itching on their snouts.

Stinging nettle

The stinging nettle was once popular with Pacific Northwest Indians, who used it as a material for making fishnets, snares, and tumplines. While Indians were also known to steam and eat the plant (resulting in its other common name, Indian spinach), this may have happened only at the instigation of settlers who were familiar with the nettle in Europe.

As a child I remember balancing on a log with friends, dressed in swimming trunks and armed with a cudgel, to reenact the famous contest between Robin Hood and Little John. Our log, rather than crossing a river as in the story, traversed a vicious patch of stinging nettles. After battling each other with long staves, one of us would ultimately tumble, nearly naked, into the nettles. I acquired a rather good sense of balance and can wield a pretty mean cudgel as a result!

8 On the far side of the point the trail winds gently back up the hill to the gate, approximately 0.8 mile from the intersection with the lower logging road.

15 Cable Trail to Rocky Point Road Hike

TRAILHEAD NW Skyline Boulevard between Moreland Road and Johnson Road

DISTANCE 4.5 miles one way, 9 miles round trip

DURATION Three hours and thirty minutes

ELEVATION A total change of 720 feet, with a low point of 580 feet and a high point of 1300 feet

CONDITIONS The logging roads on this hike are mostly maintained and graveled, but some are partially overgrown, and there is one slippery, rutted descent from the highest point. There are no paths or thickets to contend with. Discarded logging cables remain in evidence on the trail from past timber harvesting.

FROM DOWNTOWN This hike begins 17.8 miles from West Burnside and Interstate 405. I recommend positioning a second car at the final waypoint, where the route runs into NW Rocky Point Road. To do this, drive north on Highway 30 (also called St. Helens Road) past Linnton, Burlington, Cornelius Pass Road, Logie Trail, and the Wildwood Golf Course. Turn left onto Rocky Point Road and follow it 1.4 miles until you reach the first gate on the left. Park one car at this gate, and then continue up Rocky Point Road in the other car until you reach NW Skyline Boulevard. Turn

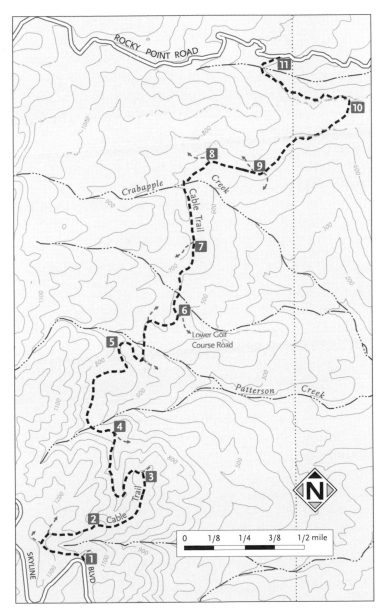

ROCKY POINT ROAD

Crabapple Creek

Cable Trail

Lower Golf
Course Road

Patterson Creek

Cable Trail

SKYLINE BLVD

N

| 0 | 1/8 | 1/4 | 3/8 | 1/2 mile |

left onto Skyline. Look for horses in the pasture on the right as you pass the Sky Ranch located at the intersection with Moreland Road. You will drive past a modern house on the left and two further gates on either side of the road just beyond the driveway. After this the road curves right and then swings to the left again. Shortly beyond this bend, the road curves sharply to the right. On the left (on the outside of this elbow curve) is a blue gate. Park your second car here.

If you prefer to take just one car, begin by turning left onto Logie Trail from Highway 30. Follow this steep, winding road up the mountainside to NW Skyline Boulevard. Turn right on Skyline and proceed north for 1.3 miles until you reach a sharp elbow curve to the left. Park near the blue gate on the right.

This remote hike along a half-hidden trail in the Crabapple Creek area takes you through young forest as well as some mature stands, with beautiful views on the way down into the basin, wide vistas across logged slopes, and majestic views of the Columbia River, Mount Hood, Mount Adams, and Mount St. Helens.

The Crabapple Creek area is a vast tract of privately managed timberland between Logie Trail to the south, Rocky Point Road to the north, Skyline Boulevard to the west, and Highway 30 to the east. The area is traversed by two year-round creeks, Crabapple and Patterson.

1 The gate at the beginning of this trail marks the only southern entrance to the Crabapple Creek watershed. It is an area with an interesting past.

While Rocky Point Road contributed to the establishment of the unique community of Dixie Mountain in the 1880s, the Logie

The view from near Rocky Point Road

Trail has a history that precedes the arrival of the Europeans. Had you walked the Logie Trail two hundred years ago you would have encountered lots of Tualatin (or Atfalati) Indians traveling between the Columbia River and the main Tualatin village, Chakepi ("Place of the Beaver"), located near present-day Beaverton. While the women might not have shocked you with their simple blouses and plaited-grass aprons, the men might have stopped you in your tracks, since they rarely wore any clothing at all through much of the warmer months.

The Logie Trail ended at the Multnomah Channel, where canoe travel provided access to Sauvie Island and the Columbia River. In hopes of benefiting from this Indian trading hub, Nathaniel Wyeth built Fort Williams on Sauvie in 1843—directly across from the trail. Unfortunately, by then disease had already reduced the Tualatin from many thousands to a mere six hundred people encamped near present-day Gaston. Six years later only sixty Indians remained, and the few survivors were eventually resettled to eastern Oregon.

Beyond the forest gate the trail splits. The right-hand trail dead-ends almost immediately, so follow the left-hand road. This track ascends gradually from the gate, at an elevation of 1200 feet, to the highest point on this hike, 1300 feet, 0.3 mile up the slope.

Near the top the road splits again. This time take the right-hand trail. The trail crests about 100 feet further along and then begins to drop gradually. Look for an overgrown, rutted path leading off to the right about a tenth of a mile past the intersection and just beyond the high point in the trail. When you spot it, leave the main trail and descend this minor tributary path.

In late winter keep your eyes open for mountain quail (*Oreortyx pictus*). Although these birds are rarely found around Portland, they reportedly frequent these remote cleared areas along the eastern flank of the Tualatin Mountains.

2 The side trail you've now entered is what I call the Cable Trail, a name inspired by the old logging cables laying in the grass across the trail. It proceeds steeply downhill, with deep ruts through overgrown vegetation. The initial portion of the descent can be slippery in wet weather, but take heart: this scramble is the most difficult part of the hike. The Cable Trail levels out at an elevation of 1070 feet, having dropped 233 feet in a mere 0.3 mile—that's a 15 percent grade!

Now the Cable Trail turns northeast and continues for another 0.3 mile through a young forest to the end of the ridge.

3 At the end of the ridge at an elevation of 1068 feet you will observe another trail spur heading off to the right. Pass it and continue along the road to the left, which leads downward for 0.4 mile to the base of the slope.

Take a moment to look out over the valley in front of you. This is the Crabapple Creek watershed, which comprises the northern half of the privately managed forestlands situated between Logie Trail to the south and Rocky Point Road to the north. Immediately to the right, south of the ridge you're standing on, a small creek cascades down the slope to become Patterson Creek. This creek comprises the southern watershed of this lovely, secluded forest basin.

4 The base of the hill lies at an elevation of 780 feet. There you'll see one spur leading off to the right and another to the left—both dead-end about 100 feet back in the woods. Continue along the main track, skirting just to the left of a thick, young conifer forest.

At this stage the road levels out for half a mile as it follows the base of the hillside, which was logged from 2002 to 2006 (and which in places is still being actively logged). These hillsides are crossed with elk and deer trails, so a quiet observer might be able to spot these animals moving among the waist-high seedlings and brush. The purple flowers of broadleaf lupine (*Lupinus latifolius*) are easier to spot, however, as they color the roadside in late summer. On warm summer days red-tailed hawks and bald eagles ride the updrafts, patrolling these slopes in search of some fast, scurrying food. In midwinter a fresh snowfall will provide ample evidence of the heavy traffic through the area. I once followed a cougar up this road after a very early morning dusting provided me with clear tracks of the cat's nocturnal passing.

5 As you approach the northern end of the hillside clear-cuts, the road enters into a downward-sloping S-bend. At the beginning of this bend you'll note a side track on the right heading off into the center of the dense replanted forest you've just circled. Continue down the main road as it twists and turns for the next 0.3 mile. In the second bend you'll encounter another side spur heading off into the woods to the right. Both spurs are dead ends.

As you come around the second bend you'll find yourself on a lovely, straight stretch of road that crosses a minor creek. This road is flanked on both sides by tall, leafy maples that provide ample shade in the summer and brilliant foliage in the fall. You may suddenly feel as though you've walked into a French Impressionist painting.

Keep a watchful eye skyward as you ascend the northern end of this verdant tunnel. When the main trail turns to the right you will note a road heading straight up the hill. This spur leads to two fine vantage points: the first one faces northeast across a clear-cut and out toward Sauvie Island, and the second one, about 100 yards further along, looks out over a clear-cut valley and provides a good view of the entire area. On one walk up the spur I was buzzed by a big baldie who presumably didn't like me in his front yard. This ten-minute detour is delightful, but keep your eyes peeled for our fine feathered friend.

6 Within about 500 feet you will reach an intersection with another strategic track. This one eventually leads down to the Wildwood Golf Course and is hereafter referred to as the Lower Golf Course Road (see the Double Cross Loop).

At this intersection take the left-hand option and continue to head north, ascending the hill from the present elevation of 620 feet. About 500 feet beyond this intersection the road crosses Crabapple Creek, which flows off these slopes and eventually runs through the Wildwood Golf Course and out to the Multnomah Channel.

As you walk further the track skirts the bottom of a large clear-cut that extends across the upper slopes of the Crabapple Creek watershed. The last portion of this clear-cut was harvested in 2005.

7 After climbing to an elevation of 750 feet in 0.4 mile from the intersection with the Lower Golf Course Road, you will encounter a logging road apparently emerging out of the clear-cut area above you and entering the Cable Trail from the left. This trail is used in the Beaver Ponds Loop.

From here the road dips down and crosses another creek as it resumes its way north toward Rocky Point Road. Flanked by mature timber, the road rises gradually until it turns eastward. Since there are few roads into this forest, this one is full of wildlife.

8 Another 0.4 mile brings you to a T-intersection. Turn right. The left-hand turn leads up the slope and is described in the Beaver Ponds Loop.

As you travel these back roads, keep an eye out for one of our most ubiquitous companions. The common raven (*Corvus corax*) is one of the most visible residents of these woods and can be distinguished from a crow by his ruffed throat, more prolonged soaring, and unmistakable guttural croak. Pacific Northwest Indians revered this bird as a powerful, aggressive trickster to whom we owe creation itself. In the wonderfully illustrated *Stories Told in Winter*, Douglas Hadley describes it thus:

> Vast were the western forest reaches, wondrous their scented halls and arches, housing a quiet to halt men's motion, demanding that all be still while it listened: then in the topmost limbs was heard the rushing spirit of the air.
>
> From the North came Tchamsen, the raven, Maker of all the world. That his people should know the sky and the earth, and should see what he had made, Raven sought light. With a glittering throng would he scatter the night, and with broad light character day.

9 At this point the Cable Trail slopes downhill gently, losing 60 feet in 0.2 mile until it reaches the intersection with a track leading to the base of Runaway Ridge. Just prior to that junction you will pass a spur leading up the hill to the left. This leads to the base of a clear-cut that can be accessed from Rocky Point Road.

The active timber management of this land provides varied environments that support a higher density of wildlife. This view was photographed from the summit of the clear-cut described in waypoint 9.

10 Continue past the road to Runaway Ridge, climbing about 100 feet in elevation to the summit of the hill that leads out of the Crabapple Creek watershed. On the way you will pass beneath a set of power lines, a terrific spot to view the entire Crabapple Creek basin.

11 From the crest of the hill (762 feet elevation) the trail to Rocky Point Road takes you through stands of nearly mature timber for 0.9 mile. You will pass beneath power lines one final time just before rounding the last bend.

You are now approaching Rocky Point Road, built by the original homesteaders on Dixie Mountain in the 1880s. For years it remained little more than a trail, but with volunteer labor it was eventually widened to accommodate wagons and buggies. Even then it remained treacherous, however—locals joked that "in the winter it was a mile deep" (Nelson and Tannock 1998). As late as the 1920s it was reported that although it only took an hour to reach Portland from this road in the summer months, the same trip took the better part of a day during the seven months of the rainy season. During county proceedings to close this challenging road, an unsympathetic judge hearing a local appeal advised the residents "to move out to civilization where there were good roads."

If you were to continue up Rocky Point Road you would encounter the northern terminus of Skyline Boulevard and a series of rural roads that connect with Scappoose to the north and Washington County to the west. The settlement of Dixie Mountain, established by John Dix and his son, is one of the most interesting communities in the area. Be sure to visit the Dixie Mountain Strawberry Festival that takes place each Father's Day—it's a unique backcountry celebration!

Over the last 4.4 miles you have covered most of the northern portion of the Crabapple and Patterson creek watersheds. This is the only known walking trail lengthwise through the area. Access to the southern portion is more difficult due to private development across the access roads and steep terrain near Logic Trail. For tips on how to access the Patterson watershed, consult the trail description for the Double Cross Loop.

(16) Beaver Ponds Loop

TRAILHEAD NW Rocky Point Road, 1.5 miles off St. Helens Road
DISTANCE 5 miles round trip
DURATION Two hours and fifteen minutes
ELEVATION A total change of 409 feet, with a low point of 654 feet and a high point of 1063 feet
CONDITIONS This loop follows graveled logging roads and a short distance of clear forest path. Between waypoints 10 and 11 the road is very rocky and somewhat overgrown with alders and occasional blackberries.

FROM DOWNTOWN This hike begins 18.5 miles from West Burnside and Interstate 405. Drive north on Highway 30 (also called St. Helens Road) past Linnton, Burlington, and the Cornelius Pass intersection. About 16 miles from downtown Portland, you will pass a truck weighing station on the right side of the highway. Immediately beyond it look for a sign indicating the junction with NW Rocky Point Road. Turn left and proceed up Rocky Point Road for 1.4 miles until you come to the first (blue) gate on the left. Park here.

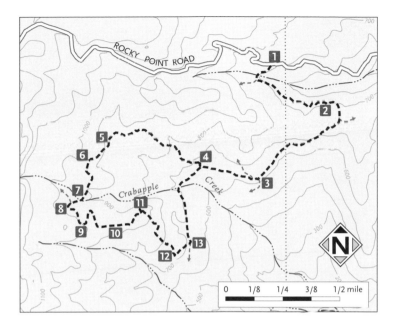

The Beaver Ponds Loop winds along logging roads past beaver ponds secluded among remote stands of a maturing forest. After slipping down a hidden trail you will emerge onto a wide vista replete with soaring eagles and mysterious black ravens who watch as you trespass through their forest.

1 Beyond the gate, walk down the logging road past another set of gate posts and follow the roughly graded road as it crosses a small creek and turns left (0.1 mile), heading east. A short spur road is visible just beyond the bend, but it leads nowhere. The road passes under a set of power lines that will serve as a reference point along the entire route.

A beaver pond secluded in the upper reaches of the Crabapple Creek watershed. Less than one minute after this picture was taken a violent hailstorm coated the pond with ice. Note the upturned tree with a Medusa-like tangle of roots extending upward from the pond's surface.

2 About 0.8 mile into the hike the road turns right (southward) and begins to ascend a ridge. Prior to crossing this divide, you will also note another track heading off to the left. This track is relevant to the Runaway Ridge Loop.

At 0.9 mile into the hike you will cross over the ridge at an altitude of 762 feet to descend into the beautiful Crabapple Creek watershed. The road proceeds gently downhill into this remote watershed, eventually passing beneath the power lines you first encountered on the north side of the ridge. Stop for a moment to catch the magnificent view from this vantage point; you can see all the way into Portland. Follow the road down the slope 0.4 mile from the crest to the next intersection.

3 This intersection presents you with a Y-split in the road. The left-hand fork leads further down into the Crabapple Creek basin and to the base of Runaway Ridge (see the Runaway Ridge Loop). On this hike, however, turn and climb the right-hand fork. Just beyond the junction another spur heads uphill. This road leads to a clear-cut hillside whose summit can easily be reached from Rocky Point Road. Ignore this upper spur and continue along the main logging road another 0.3 mile to the next junction.

4 At the next intersection the main road appears to turn left and proceed downhill in a southerly direction. You will be returning by this route, but for now proceed straight ahead, climbing the slope in front of you. Starting at an elevation of 725 feet, the road ascends for the next half mile at a 10 percent grade. As you climb you will pass through some remote forests that harbor considerable wildlife, from hawks and deer to rough-skinned newts and grouse.

You will also pass two beaver ponds that are clearly visible from the road. These are technically sag ponds, a common feature in landslide topography, and have been further dammed by the logging road that runs across them. The beavers, however, have made these ponds their own by assiduously blocking the outlets and building their lodges deep in the water. Forest managers patrol these ponds to control beaver activity, which poses a threat to the logging roads.

5 After the half-mile climb, at an altitude of just over 900 feet, you will arrive at the first beaver pond, now a boggy depression on the uphill side of the road. This was a fairly large pond when it was still occupied by a beaver.

6 In another 0.1 mile you will pass a spur leading uphill. This one dead-ends in the forest about 100 feet higher in elevation. The road dips here, and 0.2 mile onward you will arrive at another drained beaver pond on the right.

7 After the second beaver pond the road begins to climb again, emerging into a large clear-cut area 0.1 mile further along.

8 The road splits here, with the main road leading upward into the clear-cut. This right-hand fork dead-ends at the base of the massive hill you see above you. For the purposes of this hike, opt for the less-traveled left-hand option, which hugs the verge of the forest.

9 After climbing this last 0.1 mile you will have reached the high point of the hike: 1063 feet in elevation. This spot affords a beautiful view into the valley. You may want to save your lunch to eat on one of the many giant stumps here, each bearing mute testimony to the mighty trees that once covered the ground. You may even spot the eagles nesting in the trees across from you on the other side of the valley.

As you return to the logging road, you will find it winding its way north along a ridgeline on the left-hand edge of the clear-cut you've been viewing.

10 Another 0.1 mile onward you will encounter two spur roads leading down into the clear-cut. They look tempting but are *not* the quickest way down. Continue to follow the rough, rocky road along the ridgeline.

11 At the far end of the ridgeline the road angles into the woods, passing through a tangle of alder seedlings that may obscure parts of the trail. Continue into the forest, pushing the alders aside (0.2 mile from the spur roads you just passed) until you emerge into a narrow clearing. As you look to the northern end of this clearing you will see the remains of a large blue tarp lying under the trees. Instead of heading north toward the tarp, turn right so that you are facing southeast. Proceed to the very edge of the wood, and when you peer among the trees you will see a narrow trail heading off from the southeast corner of the clearing. Follow that trail, which will quickly lead to an unmistakable path that passes under the dense trees like a tunnel.

Follow this hidden trail down 0.3 mile. It parallels the clearcut valley just inside the forested area, steadily dropping altitude until it comes out into a small copse of deciduous trees on somewhat flat ground.

12 Wend your way through these trees and you'll suddenly emerge onto another logging road. This is an access road to the lower portion of the clear-cut valley—immediately to the right. Follow this road 500 feet to the left, to where it intersects with the main road (the Cable Trail) that traverses the entire Crabapple Creek basin.

13 Turn left onto this well-traveled gravel road, which in 0.4 mile returns you to the intersection described at waypoint 4. From here you merely need to retrace your steps along the logging road that was used to enter the basin.

⑰ Double Cross Loop

TRAILHEAD NW Skyline Boulevard between Moreland Road and Johnson Road

DISTANCE 5.4 miles round trip

DURATION Three hours and thirty minutes

ELEVATION A total change of 1000 feet, with a low point of 300 feet and a high point of 1300 feet

CONDITIONS This is the most challenging hike of those I've described in the northern Tualatin Mountains. Not only does the elevation change by more than 1000 feet, but the hike includes some steep descents, an extensive (0.4 mile) bushwhack trail, and at least two creek crossings. It is a demanding trail and one I would recommend for a warmer, drier day, since the heavy foliage is likely to soak your pants and boots in wet weather. It may be helpful to wear long pants and bring along rose pruners for the bushwhack trail.

FROM DOWNTOWN This hike begins 17.8 miles from West Burnside and Interstate 405. Drive north on Highway 30 (also called St. Helens Road) past Linnton, Burlington, and the Cornelius Pass intersection. About 13.5 miles from downtown Portland, you will see a sign for Logie Trail on the left. Take this steep, winding road up the mountain to reach NW Skyline Boulevard. Turn right on

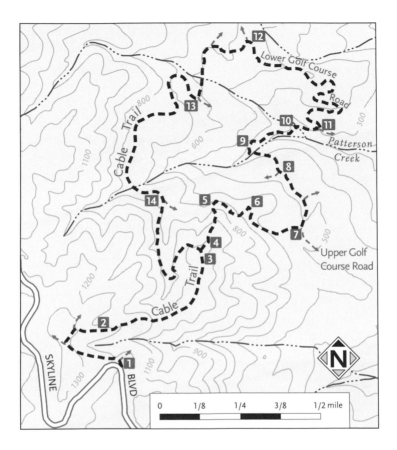

Skyline Boulevard and proceed north for 1.3 miles until you reach a sharp elbow curve to the left. On the right is a blue gate heading into a young conifer forest. Park near this gate.

The Double Cross Loop takes you into an almost inaccessible portion of the Crabapple and Patterson creek watersheds. It is the only way to access this remote area on a day hike; alternative routes would require at least 4 miles of hiking to even approach the area. Part of this loop uses the Cable Trail (see the Cable Trail to Rocky Point Road Hike). It is a strenuous hike, but one that takes you deep into the Crabapple Creek basin, along long-abandoned roads, down misty ridgelines with spectacular views, past forests full of wildlife, and across a number of small but active creeks. When I really want to get off the grid, this is one of my favorite hikes. Plus it's a very good work-out! Take your time and enjoy this spectacular hike as it loops through an area otherwise too remote for day hikers.

1 The trail splits just beyond the gate. Take the left-hand option, which climbs gradually from an elevation of 1200 feet to 1300 feet, the highest point on the hike, in 0.3 mile. When the road splits again, take the right-hand trail. This trail crests about 100 feet further along, then begins to drop. Look for a side trail leading off to the right about a tenth of a mile past the intersection and just beyond the high point in the trail.

Rough-skinned newts are a common sight for Northwest hikers.

2 This rutted, overgrown side trail is the Cable Trail, which continues steeply downhill (and which can be slippery in places, so be cautious in rainy weather). This trail levels out at 1070 feet elevation after having dropped 230 feet.

Turning northeast now, the Cable Trail continues for another 0.3 mile through a young forest to the end of the ridge, from where you can get a great view of the Crabapple Creek basin and this trail winding down into the forested bowl. On your way to this point you will notice an old logging cable lying in the grass across the trail

3 As you reach the end of the ridge (1068 feet elevation) you will notice another trail spur heading off to the right. While the main trail on the left continues down the slope, the side trail, overgrown with wild grasses, heads northeast to end in a cul-de-sac a short distance further. Choose this right-hand option and proceed 0.1 mile to the dead end.

4 Standing at the conclusion of the trail you will observe an almost solid wall of trees. Note carefully on the left-hand side a small break in the trees and a path passing neatly between the low-hanging branches. You can recognize the path by the fact that it emerges on the other side of these woods into an area of slightly younger trees. Immediately to the right a wall of taller trees marks the edge of an earlier clear-cut. This bushwhack trail skirts the edge of the older forest as it descends the ridgeline down to an old skidder road (where earthmoving vehicles cut rudimentary tracks into the slope to provide access for loggers and their equipment)—0.2 mile down the slope.

Throughout this thickly wooded section the trail is marked by blue yarn tied at intervals and hanging from trees, stumps, and overhead branches. Cutting through waist-high salal and slipping in and out of young fir trees, the trail descends along a wall of older trees to the right. Keep a close watch for where the branches have been trimmed back and where the Oregon grape, salal, and occasional blackberries have been trimmed. Near the bottom of this steep descent the trail switches back and forth among the trees as it navigates the final drop to the older skidder road at the base of the ridge. The last few feet down are strewn with rocks and fallen branches. Step through these and you will see that you've arrived at a ledge that is, in fact, a skidder road leading down and to the right.

5 This skidder road is recognizable because it forms a ledge of level ground, albeit overgrown with dense conifers. A dark, shaded passage slips between the clipped trees and leads down to the right for 0.2 mile. Follow this sylvan tunnel around the occasional batch of blackberry vines struggling to survive in the conifer gloom. The yarn will continue to guide you. Eventually the road departs from its transverse direction along the hillside and turns to slip down the slope, following a steeper track until it emerges 50 feet later at the very end of a remote logging road. Using this bushwhack route down from the Cable Trail, you've now penetrated into the heart of the Crabapple Creek basin. It would take many hours to get to this point following the labyrinthine logging roads, and using this shortcut you've done it in less than ninety minutes.

6 You're now on a wide, roughly surfaced gravel logging road. Directly ahead is a dead-end spur, but if you follow the road 0.2 mile to the right it will skirt the bottom of a large cliff and drop down to an intersection with another more heavily used road that leads to the golf course (left) and into the Patterson Creek watershed (right). I refer to this as the Upper Golf Course Road; it eventually connects with the Lower Golf Course Road (see also the

Cable Trail to Rocky Point Road Hike) near the entrance to the golf course itself.

7 Turn left once you reach the Upper Golf Course Road and proceed down about 350 feet. There the road splits again, with the main track heading off to the right. Choose the left-hand turn and continue to traverse the slope in a northerly direction for another 0.2 mile.

8 At this point you will encounter another split in the road. Turn right, heading down the slope. The road begins to turn into a track, with moss and grass replacing the gravel. As the track drops to an elevation of 385 feet it becomes rougher, occasionally blocked by fallen trees, berms, and ditches. Climb over these and in another 0.1 mile you will reach the first major creek crossing.

9 Before crossing the creek you must surmount a large, overgrown berm. The watercourse itself is in a narrow gorge that cuts through the track, about 4–5 feet below the surrounding terrain. The uphill side of the streambed is narrow enough to jump across, but dogs will have to clamber down and scramble up the far side (and some may require assistance to climb up the opposing bank). On the far side of this first crossing, the trail continues along the old road for 0.3 mile, crossing several smaller berms and easily surmountable smaller watercourses.

10 The second big crossing is similar to the first. Here, too, an initial berm must be crossed, after which you're obliged to descend through a thicket of alder seedlings to the edge of the watercourse. This creek is larger than the first and requires descending into the streambed, a 4-foot drop from the lip of the ravine. You and your companions will again need to pull yourselves up the far side. (I don't recommend doing this during one of Oregon's infamous downpours.)

11 Having navigated the second and last crossing of these unnamed tributaries of Patterson Creek, you will be within 500 feet of the intersection of this disused track and the well-maintained road that ascends from the Wildwood Golf Course. I refer to this road as the Lower Golf Course Road. Although the last few yards of the track pass through an area sprouting blackberry bushes, it is relatively free of ensnaring tendrils that might hamper passage. Turn left onto the Lower Golf Course Road and begin to ascend the hill.

12 The Lower Golf Course Road twists and turns its way upward, eventually traversing a ridge that divides the Crabapple Creek watershed from the watercourses that flow into Patterson Creek. In all, the ascent up this road to its intersection with the Cable Trail covers 0.6 mile. About half a mile up the road you will encounter a spur on the right that leads down the northern slope of the aforementioned ridge and crosses Crabapple Creek 0.3 mile northward.

Turn left at this intersection. You are now on the Cable Trail, which is even more well maintained than the Lower Golf Course Road, with evidence of frequent vehicular travel. Only 200 feet further you will spot a road heading straight up the hill to the right. This spur, also described in the Cable Trail to Rocky Point Road Hike, leads to two excellent viewpoints. The first spot looks across a clear-cut toward Sauvie Island, while the second looks out across the entire area.

As the Cable Trail turns to the left, heading south, you will drop down onto a charming, maple-edged road that runs across a small creek.

13 At the far end of this lovely stretch, the road begins to climb into a series of S-bends that will elevate you to the base of the higher slopes. In these bends you will encounter two spur trails leading off on the left into the densely replanted conifer forest. Both are dead ends. Remain on the main road, which ascends for 0.3 mile to an open area that often provides glimpses of elk or deer traversing the recently logged slopes above. Upon passing the second spur trail, take a moment to look straight down the corridor. In the distance you will see a forested ridge; it is the same ridge you descended using the rough bushwhack trail.

14 Proceed onward about half a mile, circling around a thickly replanted forest at the base of the Crabapple Creek basin's upper slopes until you reach the next spur leading off to the left. At this point the main road turns to the right, and you will begin to climb upward from an elevation of 780 feet. Almost immediately you will encounter another spur road splitting off to the right, but it is clearly a secondary road; ignore it as you begin the long climb to the end of the ridge at an elevation of 1068 feet.

The hike up to the end of the ridge is 0.4 mile long and bends in and out of a narrow ravine. The area around the trail is steep and full of wildlife, including raptors, who like to sit in a tree overlooking the road. Take your time ascending this portion of the trail, as the elevation gain is nearly 300 feet in less than half a mile.

Once you arrive at the top you will have completed the circuit to reach the upper portion of the Cable Trail. At the intersection that marks the end of the ridge, turn right. The left-hand spur is the one you took to descend into the valley.

From here it's merely a job of retracing your steps along the ridge, up the steep scramble to the top of the hill, around a couple of left-hand turns, and back to the gate on Skyline Boulevard.

(18) Runaway Ridge Loop

TRAILHEAD NW Rocky Point Road, 1.5 miles off St. Helens Road

DISTANCE 3.4 miles round trip

DURATION One hour and thirty minutes

ELEVATION A total change of 425 feet, with a low point of 340 feet and a high point of 765 feet

CONDITIONS This loop follows logging roads that are mostly well maintained. A short portion consists of a path that winds through a thick stand of young conifers, emerging into a small clearing among older trees. The path is clearly visible as it winds through ferns and underbrush before it reaches a large, well-maintained logging road.

FROM DOWNTOWN This hike begins 18.5 miles from West Burnside and Interstate 405. Drive north on Highway 30 (also called St. Helens Road) past Linnton, Burlington, and the Cornelius Pass intersection. About 16 miles from downtown Portland, you will pass a truck weighing station on the right side of the highway. Immediately beyond it look for a sign indicating the junction with NW Rocky Point Road. Turn left and proceed up Rocky Point Road for 1.4 miles until you come to the first gate on the left.

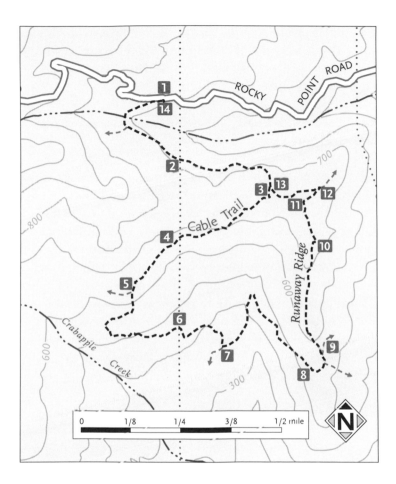

This is a great introduction to the beautiful seclusion of the Crabapple Creek watershed. It traverses a long ridge (which I call Runaway Ridge in reference to my dog's occasional independent streaks) that slopes down into the watershed and winds around the isolated forest lanes. Although it feels like the remotest corner of Oregon, it is a mere half hour from downtown.

1 From the gate, follow the logging road as it passes another set of gate posts and heads east (0.1 mile). A creek passes under the road in a culvert but is not really visible. The first spur off to the right is a cul-de-sac.

2 The power lines above you here will serve as a reference point along the entire route.

3 About half a mile into the hike the trail turns right, now heading south, and ascends to cross the ridge it has been traversing. At this point you will note another track heading off to the left. This is the track on which you will return at the end of the hike. For now, bypass it and cross over the ridge (762 feet elevation) to descend into the beautiful Crabapple Creek watershed on the main road.

4 The logging road is easy to follow as it descends into this remote watershed, eventually passing under the power lines encountered earlier in the hike. Stop here to enjoy a magnificent view of the Tualatin Mountains and the distant bridges of Portland.

5 At an altitude of about 650 feet, 1.1 miles into the hike, the road splits. Take the left-hand track as it continues to descend into the valley. The main track heads to the right and proceeds much deeper into this isolated area. (For more options in the Crabapple Creek watershed, see the Cable Trail to Rocky Point Road Hike, the Beaver Ponds Loop, and the Double Cross Loop.)

6 As the road heads back in an easterly direction, you will once again pass beneath the power lines. You are now 1.5 miles into the hike.

7 This secluded forest lane twists and turns along the gentle hillside. At an elevation of 370 feet, 1.7 miles into the hike, you will pass another side trail heading downhill on the right. This side trail dead-ends further down the slope without connecting to the golf course at the base of the slope or to any other trails. Continue along the main track, which drops to an elevation of 360 feet just beyond this intersection. Thereafter the track begins to climb as it mounts the ridgeline.

8 At 540 feet elevation, 2.1 miles into the hike, you will encounter the next trail leading off to the right. This trail heads down the ridgeline (as if it connects with the Wildwood Golf Course, whereas in reality it lands in a bramble patch lower down on the slope). Yet again, remain on the main track and stay left. Very shortly the trail will curve around and begin to head further up the ridgeline.

9 Just past this eastern extremity of the hike, at the lower end of the ridge, you will encounter another tempting side spur to the right. Stay left and continue to climb Runaway Ridge. The side trail is another of the many cul-de-sacs on the ridge; it leads partway down the easterly slope before terminating abruptly in a forest of thick, young conifers. This part of the watershed is heavily populated with wildlife, including deer, coyotes, and even occasionally cougars. Don't worry, though: coyotes and cougars are unlikely to hurt you unless they are antagonized. If you see either of these animals, consider yourself lucky.

As you climb this lovely wooded ridge you will see at least two sizable anthills to the right of the track constructed by alpine ants (*Formica neorufibarbis*). These foragers are always active, running along the forest floor and all over neighboring plants and trees. Their ant piles can reach 4–5 feet tall. The anthills on Runaway Ridge were probably constructed around the time the area was originally logged, perhaps in the 1970s. This isn't anything unusual, however: I've seen anthills in Europe known to be more than five hundred years old!

You may also notice some of the mushrooms that populate this misty ridge. I have spotted numerous blue-staining boletes (*Gyroporus cyanescens*) growing in the middle of the track.

10 The walk up the ridge is less than half a mile and ends in one of those typical logging road cul-de-sacs. Here, at 2.5 miles into the hike, the trail brings you to the end of the road, near the top of Runaway Ridge at an elevation of 760 feet. Don't panic. Carefully examine the left-hand side of the clearing you're in, and under the

An anthill on Runaway Ridge

trees you'll discover an older trail leading off to the left. Follow this trail into the woods, dodging the branches that reach across it. It will lead you 0.2 mile, generally uphill, to the crest of the ridge.

11 At this point the path winds through a young forest, past a small clearing, and into stands of taller trees. Follow the clearly visible trail through these clearings as you enter a more mature and open forest.

12 At 2.7 miles into the hike the path emerges onto a logging road (760 feet elevation), with the road running directly across the path just past the crest of the ridge. The undergrowth in this more mature portion of the forest has been cleared, so if you just keep moving uphill, you can't miss the road just beyond the crest. Follow the logging road to the left.

13 A mere 100 yards onward this road intersects with the road used to enter the area. Turn right and follow the road back to the gate.

(19) Elbow Ridge View Hike

TRAILHEAD NW Skyline Boulevard between Moreland Road and Johnson Road

DISTANCE 1 mile one way, 2 miles round trip

DURATION Thirty minutes

ELEVATION A total change of 170 feet, with a low point of 1180 feet and a high point of 1350 feet

CONDITIONS A well-maintained forest road gives way to a clearly marked footpath through the woods, which in turn connects to another maintained forest road.

FROM DOWNTOWN This hike begins 17.8 miles from West Burnside and Interstate 405. Drive north on Highway 30 (also called St. Helens Road) past Linnton, Burlington, and the Cornelius Pass intersection. About 13.5 miles from downtown Portland, you will see a sign for Logie Trail on the left. Take this steep, winding road up the mountainside to reach NW Skyline Boulevard. Turn right on Skyline Boulevard and proceed north for 1.3 miles until you reach a sharp elbow curve to the left. On the right is a blue gate heading into a young conifer forest. Park near this gate.

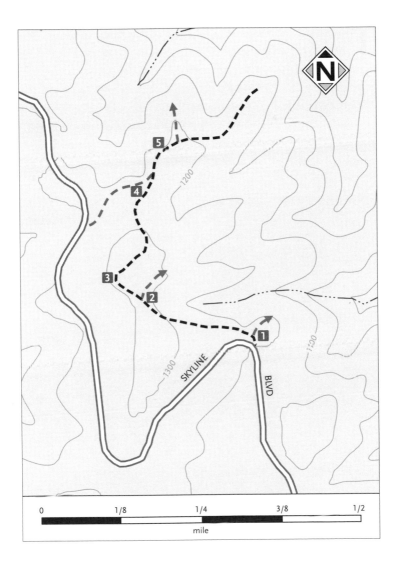

This lovely, short hike along the top of the Tualatin Mountains offers stunning views of four major mountains lined up across the horizon—it doesn't get any more Pacific Northwestish! It's a great walk to introduce visitors to the rugged beauty of our forests and the volcanic grandeur of the Cascades. The trail runs through some young woods and emerges onto a promontory with a magnificent view of the Crabapple Creek basin, Mount Rainier, Mount St. Helens, Mount Adams, and Mount Hood.

Follow this broad woodland tract to the end. Once there you'll spot the hidden trail on the right.

1 Beyond the gate, the trail splits. The right-hand trail dead-ends almost immediately, so follow the left-hand road. This track ascends gradually from 1200 feet elevation at the gate to 1300 feet about a quarter of a mile up the slope.

2 Near the top of the slope the road splits again. This time proceed straight ahead, ignoring the larger trail that branches off to the right. The right-hand option dead-ends further along, although along the way is the entrance to the semi-hidden side trail that leads into the Crabapple Creek basin (see the Cable Trail to Rocky Point Road Hike and the Double Cross Loop).

If you're hiking this trail in late winter you might spot the mountain quail that frequent the area. In fact this is an inventory spot for local ornithologists.

3 The broad woodland track continues straight for another 0.1 mile and then appears to end abruptly. However, when you arrive at the cul-de-sac you'll see that there is a small trail wending its way into the forest on the right. Follow this trail.

4 This bridle trail—which you'll be able to identify as such by the hoof marks and by the branches that have been trimmed back to accommodate riders—winds through a short patch of young conifer forest for about a tenth of a mile.

You may notice that the trunks of some of the young trees here are bald in spots. This is where the deer rub their antlers. Antlers are made entirely of bone, unlike horns, which are composed of a bony core, a layer of skin, and a layer of keratin, the tough protein found in our own fingernails. Male deer, the only animals with antlers, shed these appendages in winter and regrow them in spring. The emerging antlers are covered with a thin layer of

fuzzy skin that is said to itch, causing the deer to rub it off on any available rough surface. Hence the damage to the trees around this trail.

5 At the far end of this young conifer forest the trail emerges onto another logging road, this one extending along the ridgeline in a northeasterly direction. This road connects with Skyline Boulevard just a short distance west of where you will emerge from the young forest. Turn right on this road and follow it to its end. Take some time to enjoy the wonderful view.

In the foreground you will see the Crabapple Creek basin and the Cable Trail winding its way north toward Rocky Point Road. Beyond this is another ridge, which serves as an eagle nesting spot. To the left is a modern house that overlooks the entire valley. In the far distance, and most impressive of all, are the magnificent peaks of Mount Rainier, Mount St. Helens, Mount Adams, and Mount Hood. The view is particularly beautiful on a winter morning, when the sun struggles to appear through the mist rising from the forests below and these grand volcanic sentinels dominate the horizon under a leaden sky.

Whenever you finally pull yourself away, simply follow the same route back to the gate on Skyline Boulevard.

Mount St. Helens bathed in the last rays of a sunset

(20) Jones Creek Hike

TRAILHEAD NW Rocky Point Road, 1.3 miles off St. Helens Road

DISTANCE 3.6 miles round trip

DURATION Two hours

ELEVATION A total change of 225 feet, with a low point of 575 feet and a high point of 800 feet

CONDITIONS This hike mostly follows a 2-mile stretch of scenic logging roads through a remote forest in various stages of maturation.

FROM DOWNTOWN This hike begins 18.2 miles from West Burnside and Interstate 405. Drive north on Highway 30 (also called St. Helens Road) past Linnton, Burlington, and the Cornelius Pass intersection. About 16 miles from downtown Portland, you will pass a truck weighing station on the right side of the highway. Immediately beyond it look for a sign indicating the junction with NW Rocky Point Road. Turn left and proceed up Rocky Point Road for 1.3 miles until you come to the first gate on the right. Park at the side of the road.

The Jones Creek Hike offers lovely forested vistas and a variety of woodlands supporting a diverse range of Northwest plants,

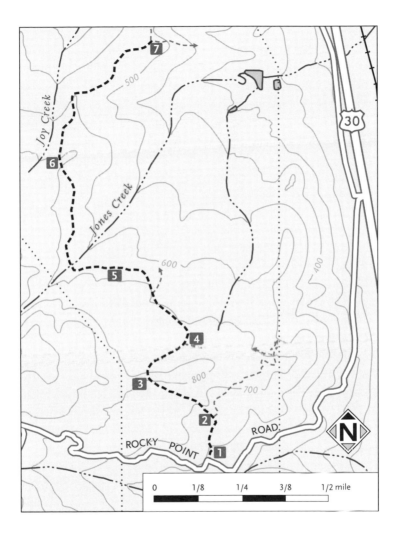

animals, and insects. The Jones Creek and Joy Creek basins are the northernmost limit of Multnomah County, and the slopes overlook the town of Scappoose in Columbia County. The area close to Rocky Point Road is used by mountain bikers who have constructed numerous side trails that crisscross the area.

1 A graveled fire lane climbs gently uphill from the gate (elevation 575 feet), heading north. Follow it about 50 feet to the first intersection.

2 The right-hand spur leads to a power-line maintenance trail that extends northward for several miles. However, the lower portions of this easement are private property, and access is forbidden.

If you do decide to take a brief detour to this ridgetop power-line maintenance track, you'll emerge from the trees at the top of the slope into a clearing under the power lines. In springtime this linear clearing is awash with foxglove (*Digitalis purpurea*), an imported European weed recognizable by its telltale bell-shaped flowers and well known as the source of the heart drug digitalis. Its evocative common name is probably derived from the Anglo-Saxon for "fox's music," a reference to two characteristics of this plant: it resembles a cluster of bells, and it grows in the scarified soil much preferred by foxes for building dens.

To the north is the burgeoning town of Scappoose. The name of this town originated from the Chinook for "gravelly plain." It was a favorite meeting place of the Columbia River "Canoe" Indians, including the Kiersinno, Clatsop, Multnomah, and Tualatin tribes, who gathered there to participate in feasts, trading, gaming, and horse races. The streams were said to be overflowing with

The Jones Creek Hike affords a nice 2-mile exploration into the extreme northern edge of Multnomah County.

salmon and the forests full of berries and wild game. At least some of this remains true, as you can witness on these remote hikes.

To avoid trespassing, however, this hike does not use the power-line easement. Instead it continues to follow the forestry road in a northwesterly direction.

3 As you ascend this road you will cross a small pass that straddles a knoll before proceeding northward. A small swamp lies on the far side of this hillock and attracts much wildlife.

It is in shady coniferous forests such as this that you will find one of our daintiest treasures, the fairy slipper (*Calypso bulbosa*), hidden deep beneath shrubs and other vegetation. This delicate, violet orchid first appears in the fall and disappears by early summer. It should go without saying, of course, but please do not pick this flower: the corm has shallow roots, and it is virtually impossible not to destroy its lifelines.

As with other members of the orchid family, the fairy slipper seed embryo develops only if penetrated, nourished, and hormonally stimulated by mycorrhizal fungi. Orchids produce as many as three or four million seeds in a single pod, but they lack a built-in food supply and have an abysmal germination rate. If it weren't for the essential intervention of the fungi, we'd have no orchids at all.

Just before waypoint 4, a spur on the right-hand side of the road leads generally in the direction of the power-line road.

4 At this point the track turns to the left. Keep an eye open for hawks and eagles as you walk down this forest-lined road. I once surprised an eagle perched directly over the road. In order to launch into flight he had to swoop off his perch and fly directly at me before gaining enough speed and loft to climb up and out of the trees. I don't know who was more surprised, the eagle or me!

5 You will spot many bike trails crisscrossing the woods on either side of the road in this portion of the forest. There is a virtual maze of bike tracks here, complete with bridges, ramps, jumps, and obstacles of every sort. You may encounter extreme cyclists during the dry season.

Follow the main track up the hillside, passing various spurs along the way. The main track is clearly evident as it wends its way through progressively older stands of trees, finally passing through medium- to older-growth timber near its highest point, around 800 feet.

6 This segment of the trail (elevation 700 feet) begins to descend toward the Joy Creek basin. As you make the descent, note the forest floor on either side of the trail, which is dark and rich in nutrients. Deep in the duff beneath the thick conifers you are likely to find some of the most unusual plants in the Northwest. One good example is Indian pipe (*Monotropa uniflora*), a short, white-stemmed plant with waxy white petals and no trace of green. Also called corpse plant or ghost plant, this small, pale plant belongs to an intriguing group known as the epiparasites.

What's so unusual about these flowers is the complex symbiotic network upon which they depend. Under these dark forest floors a vast underground web of mycorrhizal fungi is bringing about a vital exchange between the mushrooms and the trees. The fungi supply the trees with water, minerals, and nitrogen from the substrate, and the trees contribute carbohydrates. Epiparasites such as Indian pipe have developed a special role in this transaction, having evolved into a sort of free rider. As these mycorrhizal associations evolved, Indian pipe shed its now unnecessary organs, like leaves and roots, and came to subsist solely through the generosity of the leaf canopy above and the fungi below. (And you thought there was no free lunch in nature.)

177

The Crabapple and Jones Creek watersheds contain a number of beaver ponds that enhance the wildlife habitat.

7 At the furthest end of this forestry road the trail splits, with two cul-de-sacs running along two parallel ridgelines. The eastern (right-hand) trail also connects to a bridle trail that descends to the lower portion of the power-line easement, but this is private land and access is prohibited. One notable feature of this eastern cul-de-sac track is an impressive anthill that is at least as old as the forest that surrounds it. It is populated by alpine ants (*Formica neorufibarbis*).

Bibliography

Arora, David. 1991. *All That the Rain Promises, and More . . . : A Hip Pocket Guide to Western Mushrooms*. Berkeley, California: Ten Speed Press.

Bradbury, Bill. *Oregon Blue Book, 2003–2004*. Salem, Oregon: Office of the Secretary of State.

Burnett, Peter H. 1880. *Recollections and Opinions of an Old Pioneer*. New York: D. Appleton and Company.

Burt, William H. 1998. *A Field Guide to Mammals: North America North of Mexico* (Peterson Field Guides). 3rd ed. Boston: Houghton Mifflin.

Christensen, Clyde M. 1970. *Common Edible Mushrooms*. Minneapolis: University of Minnesota Press.

Crutchfield, James A. 1994. *It Happened in Oregon*. Helena, Montana: Falcon.

Davis, James Luther. 2008. *The Northwest Nature Guide*. Portland: Timber Press.

DiVincenzo, Richard J. 2002. *Linnton: A Town Too Tough to Die*. Typescript. Portland: Linnton Community Center.

Dunegan, Lizann. 2004. *Best Easy Day Hikes: Portland, Oregon*. Guilford, Connecticut: Falcon.

Edwards, Margaret Watt, ed. 1973. *Land of the Multnomahs:*

Sketches and Stories of Early Oregon. Portland: Binford and
Mort.

Fitchen, John. 2004. *Birding Portland and Multnomah County.*
Portland: Catalyst Publications.

Foster, Laura O. 2005. *Portland Hill Walks.* Portland: Timber
Press.

Friedman, Ralph. 1990. *In Search of Western Oregon.* Caldwell,
Idaho: Caxton Printers.

Friends of Forest Park. 2003. *Hiking and Running Guide to Forest
Park: Ten-Map Set.* Portland: Friends of Forest Park.

Gail's Guides. 2006. *The Famous Oregon Events Guide.* Vancouver,
Washington: Gail's Guides.

Gulick, Bill. 1991. *Roadside History of Oregon.* Missoula, Montana:
Mountain Press.

Hadley, Douglas. 1979. *Stories Told in Winter.* Forest Grove,
Oregon: Champoeg Press.

Halfpenny, James C. 1999. *Scats and Tracks of the Pacific Coast,
Including British Columbia: A Field Guide to the Signs of 70
Wildlife Species.* Helena, Montana: Falcon.

Hall, Ian R., Steven L. Stephenson, Peter K. Buchanan, Wang Yun,
and Anthony L. J. Cole. 2003. *Edible and Poisonous Mushrooms
of the World.* Portland: Timber Press.

Haggard, Peter, and Judy Haggard. 2006. *Insects of the Pacific
Northwest: A Timber Press Field Guide.* Portland: Timber Press.

Horn, Elizabeth L. 1972. *Wildflowers 1: The Cascades.* Beaverton,
Oregon: Touchstone Press.

Houle, Marcy Cottrell. 1996. *One City's Wilderness: Portland's
Forest Park.* 2nd ed. Portland: Oregon Historical Society.

Jason, Dan, and Nancy Jason. 1972. *Some Useful Wild Plants.* 2nd
ed. Vancouver, British Columbia: Talonbooks.

Jolley, Russ. 1988. *Wildflowers of the Columbia Gorge: A*

Comprehensive Field Guide. Portland: Oregon Historical Society.

Lange, Morton, and F. Bayard Hora. 1965. *Collins Guide to Mushrooms and Toadstools.* 2nd ed. New York: William Collins.

Larrison, Earl J. 1976. *Mammals of the Northwest: Washington, Oregon, Idaho, and British Columbia.* Seattle Audubon Society.

Lincoff, Gary. 1981. *National Audubon Society Field Guide to North American Mushrooms.* National Audubon Society Field Guide. New York: Alfred A. Knopf.

Lowe, Don, and Roberta Lowe. 1969. *100 Oregon Hiking Trails.* Beaverton, Oregon: Touchstone Press.

MacColl, E. Kimbark. 1976. *The Shaping of a City: Business and Politics in Portland, Oregon, 1885–1915.* Portland: Georgian Press.

MacColl, E. Kimbark. 1979. *The Growth of a City: Power and Politics in Portland, Oregon, 1915–1950.* Portland: Georgian Press.

Mathews, Daniel. 1999. *Cascade Olympic Natural History: A Trailside Reference.* 2nd ed. Portland: Raven Editions.

McArthur, Lewis A. 2003. *Oregon Geographic Names.* Portland: Oregon Historical Society.

McKenny, Margaret. 1971. *The Savory Mushroom.* Seattle: University of Washington Press.

Miller, Emma Gene. 1958. *Clatsop County, Oregon: A History.* Portland: Binfords and Mort.

Munger, Thornton T. 1998. *History of Portland's Forest Park.* 50th anniversary ed. Portland: Friends of Forest Park, 1960.

Murphey, Edith Van Allen. 1959. *Indian Uses of Native Plants.* Fort Bragg, California: Mendocino County Historical Society.

Nehls, Harry B. 1989. *Familiar Birds of the Northwest.* 3rd ed. Portland Audubon Society.

Nelson, Jack E., and Jo Ann Tannock. 1998. *Dixie Mountain Legacies: Rural Life in an Oregon Community.* Hillsboro, Oregon: Dixie Mountain Grange.

Oates, David. 2006. *City Limits: Walking Portland's Boundary.* Corvallis, Oregon: Oregon State University Press.

O'Donnell, Terence. 1988. *That Balance So Rare: The Story of Oregon.* Portland: Oregon Historical Society Press.

Oregon Health and Science University. 2003. *OHSU at a Glance.* Portland: Oregon Health and Science University.

Peterson, Roger Tory. 1998. *Western Birds.* 3rd ed. Boston: Houghton Mifflin.

Petrides, George A. 1958. *A Field Guide to Trees and Shrubs* (Peterson Field Guides). Boston: Houghton Mifflin.

Pojar, Jim, and Andy Mackinnon, eds. 1994. *Plants of the Pacific Northwest Coast: Washington, Oregon, British Columbia and Alaska.* Revised ed. Vancouver, British Columbia: Lone Pine.

Price, Larry W. 1987. *Portland's Changing Landscape.* Portland: Department of Geology, Portland State University.

Rezendes, Paul. 1999. *Tracking and the Art of Seeing: How to Read Animal Tracks and Signs.* 2nd ed. New York: HarperCollins.

Robbins, William G. 2004. *Landscapes of Conflict: The Oregon Story, 1940–2000.* Seattle: University of Washington Press.

Robinson, Peggy. 1978. *The Portland Walkbook.* Portland: Victoria House.

Schalkwijk-Barendsen, Helene M. E. 1994. *Mushrooms of Northwest North America.* Edmonton, Alberta: Lone Pine.

Sibley, David Allen. 2003. *The Sibley Field Guide to Birds of Western North America.* New York: Chanticleer Press.

Sullivan, William L. 2002. *Exploring Oregon's Wild Areas.* 3rd ed. Seattle: Mountaineers Books.

Sullivan, William L. 2006. *100 Hikes in Northwest Oregon and Southwest Washington.* 3rd ed. Eugene, Oregon: Navillus Press.

Tudge, Colin. 2006. *The Tree: A Natural History of What Trees Are, How They Live, and Why They Matter.* New York: Crown Publishers.

Turner, Mark, and Phyllis Gustafson. 2006. *Wildflowers of the Pacific Northwest: A Timber Press Field Guide.* Portland: Timber Press.

Underhill, J. E. 1974. *Wild Berries of the Pacific Northwest.* Saanichton, British Columbia: Hancock House.

Walker, Dale L. 2000 *Pacific Destiny: The Three-Century Journey to the Oregon Country.* New York: Forge.

Whitman, Ann H., ed. 1986. *Familiar Trees of North America: West.* National Audubon Society Pocket Guide. New York: Alfred A. Knopf.

Wuerthner, George. 2001. *Oregon's Best Wildflower Hikes: Northwest Region.* Englewood, Colorado: Westcliffe Publishers.

Index

Photo by Martin Flatz

About the Author

James D. Thayer was president of the Friends of Forest Park at a time when the organization grew to prominence through advocacy, focusing on trying to preserve unimpeded wildlife access by purchasing strategic parcels inside and beyond the park. Thayer has surveyed over 60 miles of trails, fire lanes, and logging roads and has mapped many trails, tracks, bushwhacks, and bramble-clogged scrambles in the Portland area.

He has served as senior manager at the Portland Development Commission and as a senior international economic development officer for the Oregon Economic and Community Development Department. In 1989 he founded the international marketing consultancy Overseas Strategic Services, helping U.S. companies find markets abroad. He has also served as president of the World Affairs Council of Oregon. Starting in 1992 he helped launch the international sales and marketing for a series of successful Oregon-based technology ventures. He serves as the president of the Southwest Hills Residential League (SWHRL) neighborhood association and sits on the board of the Portland-Bologna Sister City Association. He earned a bachelor's degree from Reed College and an MBA from the Thunderbird School of Global Management.